BOZOS, MONSTERS AND WHIZ-BANGS

BAD ADVICE FROM FINANCIAL ADVISORS AND HOW TO AVOID IT!

LORRAINE ELL

Bozos, Monsters and Whiz-bangs: Bad advice from financial advisors and how to avoid it! / Lorraine Ell, Excellat Publishing

For permission requests, email the author, addressed "Attention: Permissions Coordinator," at lorraine@bettermoneydecisions.com
(844) 507-0961 ex: 701 www.bettermoneydeccisions.com

Printed in the United States of America

ISBN 978-0-9861398-9-5

1. Financial Planning 2. Investing 3. Financial Advice
15 14 13 12 11 10 / 10 9 8 7 6 5 4 3 2 1

ACKNOWLEDGEMENTS

I would like to thank the many people who helped make this book possible: to all who spent time discussing, editing, commenting, researching, writing and contributing.

My sincere appreciation to Tony Termini whose tireless work in researching, writing and editing gave depth and humor to this work and enabled my voice to shine full force.

Many thanks to my husband George, who spent hours discussing the themes of the book and helping me express the importance of doing the right thing for clients.

Also, this book would not have been possible without the anecdotes told to me by my clients who have entrusted me with their financial wellbeing. I hope to continue to provide the highest level of guidance so that their lives are enriched by working with me.

TABLE OF CONTENTS

PREFACE

I HAVE MET numerous people over the course of my more than 30-year career in the investment business. And, I am still amazed at the stories many of them have shared – and still share – with me about their previous advisors. Those stories compelled me to write this book. They have been gleaned from conversations with clients over the years and are intended to illustrate some of the pitfalls that come with choosing the wrong financial advisor.

This book is both a cautionary tale and a "How To" book. It includes examples of what to watch out for when looking for a financial advisor and offers suggestions on how to go about selecting a suitable one. The stories illustrated here are intended to get investors thinking about how to approach the types of financial decisions they will likely face throughout their lives. I also want to use this book as an outreach to other advisors throughout the country to reconsider what they do for their clients.

My work in the financial services industry started in the 1980s. I began my career, as many in my profession did, back then. My first job was as a stockbroker, starting at Drexel Burnham Lambert, the scrappy investment bank made famous for financing some of the most notable leveraged buyouts of the time. From there I went to work at a small regional brokerage in Boca Raton, Florida. I left the brokerage business altogether in 1989.

After some time off, I traded in my life as a commission-based salesperson for one as a fee-based advisor. I went from being paid for selling products to being paid for offering clients unbiased advice and counsel. That felt pretty good! I started this new chapter in my career at a small independent firm and I stayed there nearly a decade until I opened a Registered Investment Advisory firm with a colleague and business partner. We started the firm in 2014. My industry experience is pretty extensive as I have seen the investment business from both sides of the fence. I like the side I'm on now better.

Many people don't know that there is a difference between a stockbroker and a registered investment advisor. But, the two are different in a lot of ways. The most significant of these is that brokers, by and large, are held to a different and lower standard than investment advisors. That is not a pejorative statement. It's just a fact. With the exception of advice related to a client's retirement plan, the only yardstick that a broker is measured by is whether or not his or her advice is "suitable" for a given client. And, there's a lot of wiggle room in what defines suitability. When I was first a broker, it meant that common stocks were appropriate for anyone who could fog a mirror. Seriously, my branch manager used to say just that! I won't belabor the point, but being paid a commission for selling a product opens up the door for all manner of conflicts of interest. By contrast, an investment advisor is a fiduciary.

The standards to which an investment advisor must adhere are much more rigorous because, by law, he or she is required to act only in the client's best interest. That means that a fiduciary may not receive commissions for investment vehicles his or her client purchases. At our firm, we see our advisory role in much broader terms than just being fiduciaries.

My vision for what an advisor should do for the clients he or she serves goes well beyond offering investment advice. My mission has been to help our clients with much more than just that. And, early on in the client/advisor relationship, we help them set expectations about our role in their financial lives. We want them to understand that they can expect more from us than they could from another advisor – of any ilk. Our role is to provide our clients with more planning, more advising, more educating, more coaching, more empowering, and more help navigating each of the various aspects of their financial decision-making. Our goal is to help our clients articulate their hopes, goals, wants, and dreams. And then help them deploy their assets efficiently, over time, in the fulfillment of those many and varied aspirations.

Our firm is called Better Money Decisions for a reason. The reason is that our role is to help our clients arrive at the optimal solution for each financial question they face in the course of living their lives. Some of these questions are of monumental importance. Some are less significant. Some are trivial. The point is that we want our clients to use us as a sounding board when they have questions about how to effectively use their money.

When a client needs help determining whether buying a new car with cash or with borrowed money is most appropriate for them, they know that they can count on us for advice. If they want to donate money to their favorite charity, we help them find the most tax-efficient way. If they want to give or loan money to the kids, we find ways to make it work so that no sibling feels he or she has been slighted. And, when the conversation turns to much bigger-picture issues, our clients know that we are there to help.

We prepare them to have the "estate conversation" with their adult children. We make sure that their health directives are in place. We help in the analysis necessary to determine whether or not long-term care insurance is necessary. And, we weigh in on their questions regarding other forms of insurance, from life and health to home and liability: never selling; always guiding.

This is the essence of what our firm delivers for clients. We wholly embrace the concept of "Investment Advisor as Fiduciary". Our approach is straightforward, open, honest, and transparent. Our fees are disclosed up-front. Our interests are aligned with our clients'. Our service and value-added proposition are relationship-based. We aim to understand our clients on a deep, holistic basis that transcends dollars and cents. Only in this way can we better guide them in making the right economic decisions that will have a long-term impact on their lives and possibly the lives of their children and grandchildren.

Our clients are usually in or nearing retirement. Although they come from various walks of life, they all have investable assets. We don't have a minimum needed to invest. But, there is not much we can do for people who do not have enough money to fund retirement. Most, but not all of our clients are female. That's not a requirement. We work with anyone who can benefit from our approach. That's why our first question to any prospective client is, "How can we help"?

I like to say that the investment part of helping clients is easy. Helping them make life's financial decisions is not. This requires a compassion for them as people and a passion for enlightening others. Over the course of my career, I have found that these are values that are not traditionally found in the investment industry. My hope is that this book will enlighten you to the possibilities of what a financial advisor can be and to encourage you to expect more!

I also hope that advisors who read this and see themselves in the stories about clients will reevaluate how they are doing business. Ours is a fantastic industry with the chance to not only do well but also do what's right for the clients.

AUTHOR'S NOTE

WHEN I WAS a kid I used to watch the TV show Dragnet. I got a kick out of watching Bill Gannon and Joe Friday interrogate people. And, I imitated them in real life. I was a very curious, inquisitive kid and in jest people would say that I would make a good detective. But, back then women weren't cops on TV…or on the streets.

Nowadays, I use that same curious, inquisitive nature to find out about people. Asking a lot of questions, listening intently, and letting them tell you their life stories is a very helpful skill for a financial advisor. I got that from Dragnet.

One of the other things I got from Dragnet I have used in this book. If you don't remember the television series, I can explain. Each episode started out with a narrator telling the audience that the stories they were about see were true, and that only the names had been changed "to protect the innocent". This book pays homage to that.

You see, the stories you are about to read are true. They describe real-life situations of real-life people. But, in addition to being inquisitive, being discreet is also a very important quality for a financial advisor to have. I couldn't just tell you stories about our firm's actual clients. So, I have disguised them. Some of them are mixed up and swapped around, so that when clients read this book, they too won't know if the references here are to them or some fictitious character. Nevertheless, you should recognize many of the people described in each chapter. They are all taken from popular fictional characters in movies or television shows that are a part of the fabric of our shared cultural experience.

I have done this to present the very serious subject matter here with a big helping of jocularity. The situations described in each chapter are real and the financial planning and investment management solutions described are the actual ones that we used to help those clients.

Our firm is dedicated to guiding our clients in achieving their personal life goals. We take that work – but not ourselves – very seriously. Life's too short not to have some fun along the way. I hope you learn a few things as you read the following pages. And, I hope you also have a good laugh every now and then.

INTRODUCTION

WHAT MATTERS MOST about money is how you use it to live the life you want. So, it matters how you decide to use the funds and where you allocate your hard-earned resources. Decisions aren't always easy, and money means more than dollars and cents. I learned this from personal experience.

I am the oldest of four girls and grew up in my parents' hometown of Pittsburgh, Pennsylvania. My mother was born there. My father's family emigrated from Italy and settled there. Both of my parents were incredible people.

My mother was bubbly, outgoing, and very protective of us. Before she and my father were married, my mother worked as a secretary in Washington, DC. While my dad graduated from high school, it is fair to say that he was self-educated. He didn't speak a word of English until he went to kindergarten. But, when I was growing up, I remember him as a voracious reader. He would consume close to a book a day. His literary appetite was for non-fiction, but he would read Shakespeare to us when we were children. A remarkably creative guy, he would act out all the parts as he read the bard's work. At bedtime, he would make up stories and do the same thing.

Before I was born, my parents lived in New York City and my

father worked in the theatre. It was the late 1940s. Money was tight so they rented a tiny apartment on 14th Street near Greenwich Village. There, my father took to remodeling the entire place. He used all reclaimed materials. I like to say that was because he was ahead of his time, but the fact that funds were limited probably had a little something to do with the decision.

In addition to designing and revamping the apartment's interior walls and layout, he also designed and built furniture that he scaled down to fit the tiny space. His efforts came to the attention of the editor of Living for Young Homemakers magazine and the apartment was featured in a four-page spread, complete with photos of mom and dad showing off their spectacular little place.

My parents decided to leave New York and return to Pittsburgh to raise a family. My mother became a stay-at-home mom and my father started his own business. He had a passion for tinkering and making things and he built a successful construction company using the skills he learned from his father. It was with this experience that my father built our dream home.

We lived in a beautiful house that was huge for six people. And, it was exquisite since my dad built it himself.

I tell you this to let you know that I led a very privileged life growing up. But at the age of 14, everything changed. As soon as we moved into our dream house, my father became seriously ill. He developed acute rheumatoid arthritis, a totally debilitating illness at that time. Today, treatments for the disease are so common that they are marketed using light-hearted, happy-go-lucky television commercials. It is a manageable ailment. Not back then. The treatments available today to mitigate the symptoms did not exist. My father's hands, the tools of his trade, became deformed, making it difficult for him to pick things up, let alone hold them for very long. His pain was incessant and made it impossible for him to work.

My mother needed work and she started a beauty shop but our family struggled financially. And, while I was just 14, I was old enough to realize the predicament we were in. I had a choice at that point. I could behave like a spoiled child and make life even more difficult for my parents – as many children at that age do. Or, I could grow up and become a helper in any way possible. I chose the latter. So, at the age of 14, I entered the workforce.

I took a job washing hair at the beauty shop. I earned minimum wage but was allowed to accept tips. With each wash, I collected twenty-five cents. Oh, did I love those tips!

I would come home each day with a pocket full of quarters in my white uniform and gleefully count out the money on my bed. I saved some of the money for college. And, I am proud to say that I was the first in my family to go to college. I used some of the money to buy things for my younger sisters; small treats like candy or a toy. Sometimes, I'd reward myself with an inexpensive trinket. But washing hair at the salon wasn't my only job.

With my mother out of the house, I took responsibility for the everyday tasks that never seemed to get done. I cooked our meals, kept the house clean, cared for my father, and helped to keep my younger sisters in line and out of mischief. It was from this experience that I learned two important lessons that have shaped my philosophy about money and life.

The first is that a change in circumstances can happen at any time and is perhaps inevitable. The second is that the emotional impact that money has on people is much more profound than its material effect. These lessons have stayed with me. They directed me as I attended college on a full scholarship. They aided me as I joyfully raised three successful sons. And, they informed my pursuits while I spent many years living abroad.

I have been guided through life with an understanding and belief that the value of money is merely in its ability to provide a means to a more important end. And, that end is whatever the holder wishes it to be. There are much more important things in life than money. That is the foundation of my work with clients and the underlying virtue of this book's message.

CHAPTER 1

NURSE BETTY & THE BURGER FLIPPER

Churning & Burning

BEFORE SHE RETIRED, Betty had been a nurse. So, that's the nickname we gave her. Whenever she'd come into the office for an appointment someone would invariably say, "Nurse Betty to the conference room, stat." Of course, I don't think anyone ever said that in front of her.

She is a lovely, energetic woman in her mid-70s with deep blue eyes and a flowing mane of mostly light brown hair with streaks of gray. Her beauty belies her age. She's graceful and elegant and her five-foot stature is a stark contrast to her enormous personality. With a keen wit and wicked intelligence, Nurse Betty is the type of person that people just want to be around. She has a habit of making everyone around her feel great. She's the salt of the earth.

Betty owns a number of rental properties in the local community. So, along with Social Security and the occasional residual check she receives for reruns (she appeared in 63 episodes of a soap opera), her rental income provides her with the means to enjoy retirement without financial worry.

When she first came to us, Betty brought her statements from the full-service brokerage firm where the account was held. After a few minutes reviewing those statements it was pretty apparent to me that her full-service broker would more aptly have been referred to as a self-serving one. The statements revealed lots of motion, but no progress. In fact, over the course of a year, in a positive market environment, Nurse Betty's investment account had actually declined in value.

"I don't understand one word that kid says to me" Betty scoffed. "None of this makes any sense," she said as she pointed to a six-inch tall stack of trade confirmations.

Brokers are required to send customers a notice every time a trade occurs in their account and Betty had a ton of them. I had never in my entire career seen a stack of confirmations as tall as Betty brought into the office that morning. Seriously, maybe after decades a typical investor might have a stack that tall, but even that might be a stretch. Betty's broker had been doing a lot of trading in her account.

I'll go into more detail on this point at the end of the chapter, but right now, it's important to note that our position is that an investment account should not be a "trading" account. But, that's clearly what Betty's was. And, there's a name for what Betty's broker was doing. It's called churning.

Churning is the frequent buying and selling of stocks or mutual funds in a customer's account. Brokers do it to generate commissions. The actual trades themselves have nothing to do with fulfilling the customer's investment objectives. But, lots of folks allow it to happen because they are told by their brokers that it will help them "beat the market"! Sadly, for many of them, churning ends up eating up so many of their assets – as they get converted into commissions for the broker – that they suffer irreparable harm. This is referred to as "Churning and Burning"

Betty's broker, Wesley Rock, was trading almost daily into and out of individual equities (stocks) based on some type of system he created.

Betty could not describe that system and I couldn't figure it out from reviewing the statements.

Wesley was about twenty-nine years old. She said he was a cute kid; thin as a rail, and an over-the-top caricature of a 1980s investment banker. His hair was perpetually greased and combed back like a hitman in a movie. His wardrobe included no fewer than nine pairs of braces, the fancy suspenders worn by guys who really don't need any help holding up their trousers. His Allen Edmonds Wingtip Oxfords appeared to undergo a daily ritual of spit-and-polish so rigorous that they reflected the sun like a discotheque strobe light.

I could just imagine Betty sitting down with Wesley and listening to his stock pitches. "Betty, this one's going to be a big star. There's a reason to love this one! This one's going to the moon!" It's always the same with guys like Wesley; especially when they really don't have a clue what they're talking about.

Wesley hadn't been in the business very long before he landed Nurse Betty's account, but he had been a long-established member of the community before becoming a broker. Wesley, you see, used to be the manager of the local Applebee's restaurant.

I don't bring this up to disparage restaurant managers; quite the contrary. I mention it only to point out that it occurred to us at the time we transferred Betty's account to our custodian that perhaps young Wesley believed that his experience flipping burgers somehow qualified him to now flip stocks.

Churning Without (The Obvious) Burning

Okay, churning a client's account is something that everyone will likely agree is bad. But, churning isn't the only way that big investment firms roll their clients to generate fees and commissions. One of the very best ways to do this is to pitch packaged investment products that over-complicate what is actually a very simple process. And, Wall Street loves making things complicated.

The volume of investment strategies coming out of lower Manhattan is relentless. It's ongoing and never-ending. Wall Street seems hell-bent on forcing change on the old-fashioned idea of just buying and holding. It seems as if a new-fangled, whiz-bang idea is floated every month. And, as soon as regulators are satisfied that these cutting-edge investment products have fully disclosed all of the risks and fees inherent in them, securities salespeople at the big investment firms eagerly unleash them onto their clients. This happens constantly in their attempt to differentiate themselves from their competition, which is actually astounding to me.

There really isn't anything that differentiates any of those firms from one another. They're in the exact same business selling the exact same thing. They all follow the exact same rules from the exact same regulators and nobody has an edge over anyone else. Another thing that surprises me is that Wall Street seems to completely ignore the fact that the more new-fangled or whiz-bangy an investment product is, the more expensive it'll be for their clients…oh, silly me, that's the whole point, isn't it?

Sadly, a client of ours once got caught up in the hyped frenzy that accompanies the launch of one of these new things. And, he dumped his entire brokerage account into it.

Eldon Pruitt is the sheriff of the county in which he lives. He's a big Santa Claus of a guy with all the cheer of the Christmas elf himself. Eldon is quiet, with a slow Louisiana drawl. But he's no yokel. He's a sharp cookie. He came to us for advice because the "money manager" he had been using wasn't "beating the market". Eldon is a proud man and felt that his investments should have been outperforming the broader market because his money was separately and exclusively managed for him by a big Wall Street money manager. Or was it?

One of my absolute favorite investment products (to hate) is the Separately Managed Account (SMA). An even more complex version of these is called a Unified Managed Account (UMA). This is what Eldon owned. An SMA or UMA is sort-of a private mutual fund you can call your own. They're different from a traditional mutual fund in a couple of ways.

A mutual fund is a collective investment pool. It aggregates the contributions of a lot of investors that put in small amounts of money, the sum total of which amounts to millions or billions of dollars. They are, in essence, a way for the common man (there are no common women, we're all exceptional) to invest in the stock market. And, because the money in a mutual fund belongs to lots of individual investors, they are subject to lots of rules, regulations, and government oversight that restrict what they can buy, sell, or hold. An SMA isn't subject to these same rules, regulations, and oversight.

And, because an SMA (or UMA) is a more newfangled, whiz-bangy concocted investment product, it allows the broker to earn a lot more in fees…which oh by the way…is the whole point of being a broker. And, they tout these types of accounts saying that they provide "diversification" to people who have a minimum of $100,000 to invest.

The pitch is that a hundred grand is not enough money for the individual investor to try to properly diversify on his or her own. That's the reason given for having a professional money manager do the job. But, the fact of the matter is that the client's portfolio ends up having small quantities of stocks bought and sold as the "professional" makes changes across the universe of each of the Separately Managed Accounts that he oversees. Typically, these types of accounts include somewhere in the neighborhood of 50 different holdings.

Seriously? That comes to less than $2,000 in each stock after you deduct fees. But, some people eat this stuff up! The justification for this is not unlike what our friend Wesley Rock was trying to achieve for Nurse Betty. These things are constructed in an attempt to "beat the market". Unfortunately, all this buying and selling diminishes portfolio returns in two ways.

The first is that those trades don't get executed for free. While the client isn't paying commissions, the trades do have real transaction costs that eat into investment performance. Those trades then produce either capital gains or capital losses. The losses are an obvious ding to performance. But, the capital gains can also be a drag. This is because they are mostly the short-term variety that gets taxed at the client's marginal rate. And, that can be as high as 39.6%. Ouch!

Now, don't confuse Separately Managed Accounts with the service provided by an investment advisor that manages a unique portfolio for separate individual and institutional clients to whom they charge a fee based on the value of the client's assets under management. An SMA is a packaged product sold by a broker or "wealth manager". They pitch these things as having the cachet of exclusivity.

"You're special! You have a professional portfolio manager handling your money. You're not in some common mutual fund that any Tom, Dick, or Harry off the street could buy. You're in an elite club!"

The reality is that SMAs are really just Wall Street's way of selling a mutual fund wrapped in a fancier package that comes with a fancier (i.e., higher) fee structure. But, the rocket science of SMAs isn't at the pinnacle of exorbitant fees. That position is reserved for what Eldon owned – the Unified Managed Account.

A UMA is a collection of SMAs and is commonly referred to as a "Fund of Funds". This term is used to make these things sound even fancier than they actually are. They are thrown together for the purpose of supposedly adding even greater diversification to the client's portfolio. To me, this begs the question: just how much diversification is enough? At a certain point at least, a few of the SMAs included in a UMA are going to overlap each other. If you think about it, there are just so many ways to gain exposure to equities. There are only so many publicly-traded companies in the world. Is it better to own them all? Is that what a UMA aims to achieve? I'm not exactly sure.

What I am sure about is that the UMA structure is a great vehicle for adding layer upon layer of fees to a client's investment portfolio. You work with a broker to help you "manage" your investments. He sells you a Unified Managed Account. The UMA manager goes out and buys a bunch of Separately Managed Accounts. Each of the guys running the various SMAs buys and sells stocks to help you "beat the market". Now, just which one of these layers of "managers" do you think is the one that doesn't get paid for his services? If you said none, you're right. This is why these things are my absolute favorite investment products… to hate.

Boiling Down Churning & Burning

Now, clearly, what Wesley was doing to Nurse Betty was bad. By comparison, a broker selling an SMA or a UMA seems almost noble! But, when you boil the two approaches down, they're pretty much the same thing: schemes designed to maximize brokerage firm profit at the expense of their clients. And, each is done in the name of "beating the market".

In my opinion, any investment scheme created with that as its stated objective is just folly. But, it's the chimera of beating the market that lures folks into situations where their accounts get actively traded.

And, while trading is a vital component of the mechanics that make our global financial system liquid and functional, it is not the same thing as investing. Trading is speculating. And, the key differences between speculating and investing are the amount of risk one takes and the duration of the holding period.

In general, the holding period of a speculation is short – in most cases one year or less. With regard to risk, most speculators will say that they will never put up more capital than they are willing to lose on any given trade, which means 100% of that trade. Now, let's consider how this is different from investing.

The holding period of an investment is typically much longer than one year. For purposes of illustration, it is well to point out that the main reason most Americans say they invest in the stock market is to "save for retirement". So, if retirement is 30 years away, maybe you should be thinking about your holding period in that context. I'll talk a bit more about this in the Addendum. The main concept I'd like you to start thinking about here is the matching of your investment horizons to your investment objectives. Now let's talk about risk.

Risk is one of the key concepts we discuss at the outset of the relationship with every new client. It was the one of the first things we talked about with Nurse Betty and when we met Eldon Pruitt. We go through a very rigorous process of defining risk and helping clients understand its various forms. Before we move on, I want to make one last point about risk and speculating.

I'm not about to suggest that you shouldn't speculate if you have a knack or affinity for it and can afford to lose 100% of whatever you put into any given trade. Speculating is fun and can be a thrill if the stock or option you purchased returns outsized gains. I just don't recommend managing your entire portfolio that way. As the saying goes, what goes up must come down and (as Nurse Betty knows) a short-term trade that goes the wrong way can have long-lasting implications.

So What Should You Do?

The advice that we gave to Nurse Betty was unique to her. So unique, in fact, that it may not be what we would advise another client in similar circumstances. The same is true with Eldon. But, there is a common thread that weaves its way through every one of our client engagements. So, let's talk about what that common thread is. It's how we view the stock market.

Let's begin with human nature. Human beings are restless things. We are not satisfied with the status quo. We're always looking for opportunity over the horizon and firmly believe that the grass is truly greener on the other side of the fence. That's why we figured out how to harness the power of fire, why we invented the wheel, and why the number of transistors per square inch on integrated circuits has doubled nearly every year since their invention. We're just fidgety that way. It's this fidgetiness that leads to innovation and why businesses keep growing. And, this is not a phenomenon that is exclusive to the United States. It's universal and it is the reason capitalism works.

With that as our foundation, it makes sense that businesses will continue to grow. As they continue to grow, they will continue to seek capital for that growth. And, investors who provide that capital will continue to be rewarded for it. Pretty simple. And, that's why stock markets have been in existence for more than four centuries and why investments in common stocks are likely to continue to make sense for the remainder of your lifetime. The way that we help our clients navigate this is also pretty simple.

While I'll spend more time on this in the Addendum, at this point it is important to discuss the basis of our investment approach, which is comprehensive financial planning. Once we truly understand our clients' financial goals, we work with them to map out the optimal way to deploy their assets in the pursuit of their goals. In nearly every case, a (usually significant) component of our clients' money ends up in equities. This is why an Investment Plan is such an important part of a Financial Plan.

Investment planning is akin to flying an airplane. Takeoff and landing are more difficult than actually flying at altitude. At takeoff, slight errors, which might be easier to correct in mid-flight, can have devastating consequences. While not so devastating, the same is true of investment planning. Errors made at the beginning can have long-lasting detrimental financial consequences. It is for this reason that our approach is to get it right at the beginning. If we do, then over the long haul, regular adjustments need only be slight and infrequent. After the client's Investment Plan is established, our continual advice is to stay the course.

The first step in our investment planning process is to help the client understand the risks of various asset classes (stocks, bonds, money market funds & cash) and then to structure a mix between them that offers the highest statistical probability of achieving the maximum long-term return possible without introducing any more risk[1] than the client would be comfortable accepting. This is commonly referred to as strategic asset allocation. This is a long-term decision.

Unless there is a change in the client's individual circumstances, the strategic asset allocation agreed upon at the beginning of the advisor/client relationship is the one to follow without caving in to some emotional rollercoaster. It is painful to see how others in a financial advisory role (mostly commission brokers) fail to see this wisdom and make moves in client accounts just to appease the investor's fears. Now, let's move on to step two in our investment-planning process.

1 Here I'm referring to the risk of a short-term loss of capital as opposed to the unique risks that are inherent in each of the separate asset classes noted in this paragraph. Those types of risk, we can't avoid. They're part of the bargain.

The next step is where we introduce our Investment Philosophy to clients. Here we show them the science behind the construction and ultimate composition of each of their individual portfolios. Our Investment Philosophy is based on the confluence of three areas of academic research: Efficient Market Hypothesis; Modern Portfolio Theory; and, the Four-Factor Model. These three components provide a scientific approach to investing using a globally diversified portfolio of stocks and bonds. Since this book is intended to be as much fun as possible, I won't bore you with a dissertation on any one of these hypotheses. Instead, I'll try to give you a no-nonsense overview of what we offer to clients every day.

The first element (Efficient Market Hypothesis) simply says that financial markets are so good at collecting and incorporating all the available relevant information related to any given security – and therefore all the securities within a specific market segment – that they nearly perfectly price those securities at any given point in time and that those prices actually reflect everything that could have an effect on their movement; up, down or sideways. In other words, you can't outsmart the market. The practical application of this theory is that a singular event of "beating the market" would be a matter of luck rather than any skill or investment strategy. Doing it consistently would be the stuff of a Tolkien novel.

There is a subset of the Efficient Market Hypothesis that we also inject into the portfolios we create for clients. We believe that broadening our clients' equity exposure to include developed international markets and emerging international markets helps us to increase their long-term investment returns while also mitigating their overall risk. The degree to which we add these two other asset classes to client portfolios is determined by the risk assessment we conduct at the beginning of the engagement. And, every one of our clients has a portfolio that lies somewhere on a theoretical continuum with no international exposure on one end and a high exposure on the other. This continuum is commonly referred to as the Efficient Frontier and it is different for each one of our clients.

The second component of our Investment Philosophy is Modern

Portfolio Theory, which is the foundation we rely on when helping a client arrive at his or her unique strategic asset allocation. Modern Portfolio Theory demonstrates that it is possible to create a portfolio that optimizes returns within a given level of risk, and that a diversified portfolio constructed with different, low-correlation (don't move in the same direction as one another) assets reduces risk over time. In other words, the biggest factor determining how risky your investment portfolio will be, is how you divide it up between different types of securities. The practical application of this is that if you get the mix right in the beginning; you don't need to fuss with it over time.

The last piece of the puzzle is the Four-Factor Model, which we use to help our clients turbocharge equity returns. The Four-Factor Model outlines four independent dimensions of investment returns. In other words, there are four things that affect how a given security will behave. And, we use these dimensional differences in conjunction with our clients' specific risk-tolerances to construct unique portfolios with varying degrees of exposure to small public companies, medium-sized public companies, and large public companies. The other dimensions we incorporate into client portfolios include a mix of "growth" and "value" equity investments as well as a mix of industrial types from relatively high-profitability industries to relatively low-profitability industries. In other words, we construct multi-cylinder growth engines for each client. The practical application of this is that our clients' portfolios generally run on a lot more than just a few cylinders. The results are portfolios that help accelerate investment returns without adding more risk to the overall mix.

Okay, that may have read like a bunch of jargon-y mumbo-jumbo. But, trust me, if you were to become a client of our firm, you'd catch on to this stuff pretty quickly. It is, as is much of the way we do business, pretty darn simple.

The Bottom Line

At some point, in evaluating the investing schemes promoted by some advisors, you must ask: "If this were so successful, why is this person talking to me? Why isn't this advisor living on some private island sipping Moët & Chandon Dom Perignon White Gold champagne?"

When it comes to investing, simpler is better.

As Paul Samuelson, the first American to win the Nobel Prize in Economics, once said, *"Investing should be more like watching paint dry or watching grass grow. If you want excitement, take $800 and go to Las Vegas."*

CHAPTER 2

BUY, SELL, REPEAT. BUY, SELL, REPEAT.

The Fear of Losing It All

STOCK MARKET DECLINES make some investors anxious. Paradoxically, stock market advances make other investors nervous. Helping clients manage their expectations and emotions is one of the most important (and difficult) tasks for any advisor, especially when markets are volatile. Exploiting them is the stock and trade of the broker. Emotion can lead people to do odd things; things they might not do in calmer circumstances. A commission-based broker understands that market advances and declines can unnerve people. That's why volatility is the broker's' friend. This is a fact that Rita MacDowell knows all too well.

Rita is a news producer at a local television station. She's a tall outgoing woman with long auburn hair and deep brown eyes. She's a deep thinker and a sucker for French poetry. Rita is pretty well-versed in current affairs. There's not much that she misses. Sadly, that keen attention to detail and understanding of her surroundings let her down during the turmoil surrounding the financial crisis that was precipitated by the burst housing bubble.

Prior to the financial crisis that lead to the "Great Recession", Rita's broker, Ned Tobolowsky, was an enthusiastic cheerleader for all things stock-market related. "Buy, buy, bing!" was his rallying cry. Sure, it was a little nerdy, but for Ned it was fitting.

Ned's passion for equities didn't wane in the late summer of 2007, when stocks hit their cyclical peak that September. He continued to encourage Rita to stay fully invested and continued to pitch new ideas to her that winter and through the next spring. But then, something in Ned changed. As summer slowly crept toward autumn and stock prices a little-quicker-than-slowly crept lower, Ned's ebullient demeanor became more sullen. The lower stocks fell, the gloomier his disposition became. Until one day, he called Rita in a nearly debilitating melancholy.

"I heard the panic in his voice," Rita recounted to us. "I could feel the fear coming through the phone. It was weird. 'Sell. Sell everything', he said. I was terrified. I thought I was going to lose it all. And, at the time his advice seemed to be the most logical and reasonable thing he had ever said to me."

It was September 15, 2008, the day that Lehman Brothers collapsed. And, Ned convinced Rita to divest nearly 100% of her holdings.

Now, in hindsight, Ned probably thought that he was the greatest stock market prognosticator of all time! After his inauspicious call to Rita, the stock market went on to lose an additional 38% of its value. Never mind that he had encouraged her to take realized losses in the neighborhood of 20%. He was probably proud that his advice kept her away from the firestorm that had burned so many other less nimble investors. To him, he had timed the market nearly perfectly!

Unfortunately, his advice stuck and Rita's concerns about the stock market were not assuaged until early 2011. By this time, the market had regained better than 40% of its value and rebounded above the level where it was when Ned made that fateful phone call. Rita missed out on all of those gains. And, again in hindsight, she would have been further ahead of the game had she simply not heeded Ned's warning three years earlier.

It was Ned's ability to read Rita's emotions and convince her to react to them that put her in that position. And, this harmed her in two meaningful ways. Taking her out of the market subjected her to real losses – losses that she was never able to recoup. His "advice" also scared her so much that she didn't get back into the market until after it had risen to a mark higher than where it had been when he convinced her to sell. In other words, Ned's advice had Rita sell low and buy high; the exact opposite of what common sense would dictate.

Sadly, Ned allowed Rita to play into her fear of losing it all and caused her to do almost just that. The good news for him was that Ned was handsomely rewarded for the advice!

The Fear of Missing Out

As Rita related the story to us, she added that the only reason that she ultimately got back into the market in 2011 was out of fear that she would miss the next rally that Ned had convinced her was right around the corner. That the corner was not turned for another 11 months was beside the point. Timing the market, as it turns out, wasn't one of Ned's strong suits.

Nevertheless, it can be very tempting to succumb to the argument for market timing. Wall Street survives on the notion that making buy or sell decisions based on a prediction of future price movements is the optimal way to grow and preserve capital. The logic is crystal clear.

It is absolutely true that if you get fully invested just as the market begins to rise from a cyclical trough and you hold on during the entirety of the rally, only to sell just as stocks reach their next cyclical break, you will not only have optimized the growth of your capital, you will have maximized it. It is also absolutely true that by moving into a 100% cash position right at the market's cyclical peak, and having zero exposure to stocks as they plummet and crash to their next cyclical tough, you will have indeed preserved all of your capital; again, not just effectively, but fully and completely!

If you are even more prescient and sell on each and every intermittent retracement within a bull market and buy on each and every intermittent advancement within a bear market, then your investment returns will be even better!

Repeating these exercises regularly and perpetually through each and every market cycle for the rest of your life is indeed the optimal way to grow and preserve capital. It totally makes sense. Why doesn't everybody do it?

The reason is that it's not doable. But, thank goodness for Wall Street and commission brokers because that's how we know it can't be done. Their ability (or at least their willingness) to try to time the market and play to their clients' fears about losing money in a down market or missing out on the opportunity of an advancing market is the stuff that dreams are made of. That those dreams are financed with their clients' hard-earned assets is beside the point. A broker can't be faulted for unwittingly giving bad advice...but he can still be paid for it!

There's Something So Familiar About This

In the strictest sense, market timing is trading and, as I suggested in the last chapter, I think that's a fool's errand. Market timing predictions are often related to economic conditions and data, technical analysis, or some other form of goofy prophecy better suited to a fantasy story about reliving the same day over and over again than to an investment policy. But, that doesn't stop individual investors, investment advisers, and professional money managers from attempting it in various forms.

I'm not going to cite any of the myriad research studies published on the ineffectiveness of trying to time the market. But, I will note that there has not been one confirmed study that remotely validates the practice. For heaven's sake, the "brightest" minds on Wall

Street can't accurately predict tops or bottoms. And, a lucky guess here and there does not an investment strategy make!

Now, consider the following. Since 1972 the broader US stock market has had 10 down years as shown in the table below (hint, they're the ones that are **bold**).

Stock Market Returns 1972 to 2016					
Year	Annual Return	Year	Annual Return	Year	Annual Return
1972	17.62%	1987	2.61%	***2002***	***-20.96%***
1973	***-18.18%***	1988	17.32%	2003	31.35%
1974	***-27.81%***	1989	28.12%	2004	12.52%
1975	37.82%	***1990***	***-6.08%***	2005	5.98%
1976	26.47%	1991	32.39%	2006	15.51%
1977	***-3.36%***	1992	9.11%	2007	5.49%
1978	8.45%	1993	10.62%	***2008***	***-37.04%***
1979	24.25%	***1994***	***-0.17%***	2009	28.70%
1980	33.15%	1995	35.79%	2010	17.09%
1981	***-4.15%***	1996	20.96%	2011	0.96%
1982	20.50%	1997	30.99%	2012	16.25%
1983	22.66%	1998	23.26%	2013	33.35%
1984	2.19%	1999	23.81%	2014	12.43%
1985	31.27%	***2000***	***-10.57%***	2015	0.29%
1986	14.57%	***2001***	***-10.97%***	2016	12.53%

Sources: AQR US MKT Factor Returns 1972-1992 (AQR Data Sets) / Vanguard Total Stock Market Index Fund (VTSMX) 1993 & Beyond.

If you just played the odds, then the table above shows you that you have a 77.27% chance of winning if you just stay the course. And, to really make the point, bear in mind that one dollar invested at the end of 1972, missing all of that year's appreciation and setting you up for the nearly 46% loss over the next two years, still grows to $70.54 by the end of 2016. Said another way, $100,000 invested in US stocks on the first trading day of January, 1973 and left alone, without rebalancing at the end of each subsequent year, and without making any further additions, would have grown to $7,054,446.00 by December 31, 2016. That's a Compound Annual Growth Rate (CAGR) of 10.28%.

But, you might argue that you weren't old enough to invest $100,000 forty-four years ago. Okay, so let's look at more recent history. The S&P 500 traded at a high of 1,471.77 on January 2, 2008.

Did you sell at the top because you "felt" the correction coming? Did you sell after your account lost 5%, 10%, or 15%?

A version of market timing was presented to me recently by a man who came in to talk about his investments. His then-current broker's strategy was to sell any investment that lost 10% of its value. My immediate response was to ask what the broker's strategy was to buy back in. He had no idea. How about you?

If you were prescient enough to sell on January 2, 2008, when did your clairvoyance tell you to buy back in? Go ahead, pick a date. Did you wait until 2009, maybe 2010? Maybe it was later than that? Now, consider the table below.

Highest Percent Moves Calendar Year 2008			
Date	Close	Net change	% Change
3/11/2008	12,156.81	416.66	3.55
3/18/2008	12,392.66	420.41	3.51
9/18/2008	11,019.69	410.03	3.86
9/30/2008	10,850.66	485.21	4.68
10/13/2008	9,387.61	936.42	11.08
10/20/2008	9,265.43	413.21	4.67
10/28/2008	9,065.12	889.35	10.88
11/13/2008	8,835.25	552.59	6.67
11/21/2008	8,046.42	494.13	6.54

Source: Google Finance

Investors who were out of the market for all of 2008 missed nine days where returns, in the aggregate, represented an increase of more than 55%. And, the market timer that missed those nine days would have fared far worse than the steady, patient investor that held firm and didn't panic.

Now, let me get back to that guy whose broker told him to sell on a 10% decline. I'm sure the advice to limit losses sounded logical at the time. It probably sounded even better in the midst the market downturn when he got the advice. But, again, when do you buy back in? The reason this gentleman came seeking my advice was because after selling in early 2016 – and not getting reinvested – he missed the year's entire 20% advance.

So What Should You Do?

Have you ever noticed that when driving in rush hour traffic, the lane to your immediate right or immediate left always seems to be moving faster than the one you're in? And then, as soon as you make the lane change, traffic comes to a standstill. Have you noticed this same phenomenon when you're in a grocery store checkout line?

It's human nature to make that switch. Doing something almost always seems more comfortable than doing nothing and moving for the sake of moving feels better than standing still. It gives us a sense of control over things that are really out of our control. Making a lane change in the grocery store or in slow traffic doesn't involve a lot of risk. Your circumstances don't change in any meaningful way regardless of whether the new lane gets you to your destination any faster or not. You still get there. That's not the case when the lane change means altering your investment plan.

The investment planning work we do for clients unfolds in the context of a larger, holistic financial plan. As such, our clients understand that these investment plans are based on the knowledge that their portfolios are to be used as vehicles that ultimately finance their future hopes, goals, wants, and dreams. Some of those objectives will be very long-term in nature. Others are expected to be achieved in just a few years. And, still others are much more immediate. The fact that we help our clients plan for these economic events is a big part of why each of them gets adequately funded.

If we tossed a monkey wrench into the mix every time the market had a hiccup, it would put many, if not all, of those goals in jeopardy. Changing your long-term investment plan – in reaction to a short-term market event – is a recipe for disaster. Changes in plans should only come as a result of conscious deliberation. This means that the only events that should alter one's financial or investment plan are those that are actually already addressed in the plan. This is because, for the most part, all life changes can be planned around in advance.

For example, we know when we're going to retire. And, we know that event is going to be the catalyst for changes in our economic circumstances. As a result, we can plan around that event. The same is true for most of the things that happen in our lives. We can even plan around the inevitability of our passing. While we can't take it with us, we can make plans for how our assets are distributed to heirs upon our death. So, really, there is nothing that a financial or investment plan can't take into consideration. The key is to not mess with it!

Even though most of life's big events are not surprises, sometimes things don't go according to plan. But, we can still plan for contingencies. And, as these changes unfold in our lives, adjustments to an investment plan can be made accordingly. The whole point of a plan is to articulate anticipated changes in our lives and structure a flexible framework that allows for smooth transitions that are not disruptive when life throws us a curveball.

The Bottom Line

Market volatility can be disconcerting. But, you should never lose sight of the fact that it's declines are always temporary. The advances are always permanent. This is why market volatility should not be a reason to make a change – of any kind – to one's long-term investment plan. This is why market timing is a loser's game. As I mentioned in Chapter One, our advice to clients is to stay the course. Just remember what legendary mutual fund manager, Peter Lynch, said about market timing:

"Far more money has been lost by investors preparing for corrections, or trying to anticipate corrections, than has been lost in corrections themselves."

CHAPTER 3

WHEN WE MET HARRY & SALLY

I'll Have What She's Having

THE BUSINESS OF creating and delivering investment products designed to "beat the market" is really the whole point of Wall Street. And, the "Street's" creativity is endless when it comes to conjuring up new ideas, themes, fads, and gimmicks to get people to buy something on the promise of striking it rich in the stock market. Enter Harry and Sally Crystal.

Harry and Sally were referred to us by Nurse Betty. Their steady careers created a substantial nest egg along with a government pension. Both are well-educated, common-sense people who are generally very well informed, so I was shocked to see their investment portfolio. Perhaps someone forgot to mention that to their former broker.

The account that Harry and Sally transferred to our firm's custodian had 21 separate mutual funds in it. When I asked them if they knew what they owned they stared at one another meekly and then looked me in the eye and simultaneously shrugged their shoulders. They had no idea. When I asked them what led them to the decision to invest in the 21 funds, their collective disposition changed dramatically!

Sally perked up beaming and proudly exclaimed that, "the New Conceptual Ideas Fund seeks to invest in the hottest new trends of the next decade," as if quoting right out of the fund's prospectus!

"What are those," I asked?

"What are what," Sally responded sheepishly?

"The hottest new trends of the next decade, what are those going to be?"

Picture yourself looking into the sky in the middle of a warm summer night in Montana (or some other sparsely populated place). Imagine gazing at the billions of twinkling stars above you. The Milky Way flowing across the sky like a river of light, appearing to be so close that you feel you could reach up and touch it. Think about how mesmerizing that sight is. Then consider what the look on your face might be at that very moment.

That was the look on Sally's face. Again, she (and oh by the way, Harry as well) had no idea.

"But, why then did you buy it?" I asked.

"A girlfriend of mine told me that she owned it. So, I called our broker and mentioned that to him and he said that I should own it too."

"Just like that? It sounds good, so I'll have what she's having. Is that how it went?"

The whole Montana stargazing look came over her face again.

Okay, in fairness, I have seen this type of situation happen a number of times. You go to a cocktail party and someone mentions something they own that has made them a bundle of money and you think, "gee, I gotta have that." But, more often than not, the reason that someone buys an investment that they really don't understand is because it gets sold to them.

This is the case with lots of mutual funds. A big part of why so many new-fangled, whiz-bangy, cleverly-named mutual funds end up in people's investment accounts is the result of a whole lot of selling. That's because there are a whole lot of funds out there. They're like belly buttons. And, the mutual fund companies know that to get brokers to sell their funds, they have to make them sexy.

There's an old adage in the brokerage business about selling boring things like mutual funds: "Don't sell the steak, sell the sizzle!" That's why fund companies market their products with sexy sounding names like the Strategic Income Opportunity Fund, the Continental Income Fund, the New Concepts Fund, or the Science & Technology Fund.

Don't get me wrong, I'm not picking a fight with any of these (real life) funds or the companies that created and sell them. My beef is that Wall Street has shoved down the throats of investors the notion that they know what's best for their clients and that the "products" they create are the proper route to take for folks to reach their ultimate financial goals.

Hogwash!

Most funds created by Wall Street investment firms come with either huge front-end sales loads, high internal expense ratios, or deferred sales charges; all of which are a drag on investment performance. That's why these things need to have their sizzle sexed up and sold. And, there's nothing more sizzling than to hear something like, "this sector is going to be hot next quarter".

Brokers love to sell sector funds. It is very common for me to hear from new clients that their former brokers told them that the reason for owning a given sector all boils down to demographics. The ones that seem to get sold the most are health care funds and consumer goods funds. The rationale goes something like this.

Healthcare stocks will always go up because the population is getting older. And, the reason it's a good idea to invest in consumer goods is that we all need toilet paper. Seriously, old people and their bowels; they may not actually be sexy or sizzling, but apparently, they get a lot of sector funds sold!

Okay, aside from the accepted truth that markets aren't logical and behave randomly over the course of any given market cycle, rationalizations such as these fail to take into account the many factors that drive the pricing for everything.

Healthcare pricing, for example, is impacted by Medicare, which covers lots of older Americans. Medicare has strict cost controls and imposes limits on the growth of companies that service the market. In addition, healthcare is subject to changes made by congress that can expand or limit one's access to care.

Consumer goods prices are subject to the whim of people's taste, trends, fads, and competition. Something that is in fashion today may not be tomorrow. And, factors that affect the prices of everything from paper to pizza include commodity supply and demand, foreign exchange rates, and the political climate. So, what's occurring demographically in the population today may not translate into corporate profits tomorrow.

This has other implications for investors, and brings me to another sizzle story I often hear from new clients about the advice of their former brokers. I can't tell you how many times I have heard a client say that the reason for buying a given fund was because the broker pitched its "great track record".

Really?

Okay, here again, I'm not going to bore you with a bunch of facts and figures. I'll just give you the condensed version. There have been numerous research studies dating back to the 1950s that have looked into the "consistency of performance" of mutual funds. Those studies have generally concluded the same thing.

Their conclusions have been that the top-performing mutual fund in any given period will not be the top-performing fund in future periods. The studies show that such performance does not continuously repeat itself. In fact, the odds of that happening are no better than one in three. Said another way, if you buy this year's top-performing mutual fund, there is a 67% chance that next year it'll be just a middle-of-the-pack performer and those odds won't improve any time after that. This is part of the reason that all mutual funds have to tell you that "past performance is not indicative of future results".

But, despite the fact that that well-worn phrase is emblazoned on the front page of every mutual fund prospectus, people just plain ignore it. This is especially the case with a fund that has a great track record. Human nature almost forces people to want to join in on the biggest winners of the previous year. And, brokers not only know this, they depend upon it to make a living.

The desire to participate in the investment vehicle that was last year's big winner is a manifestation of reactive investing. The elation one feels as the market trends higher often triggers the desire to buy as the fear of missing out takes control. Stocks, it is said, are the only things people will avoid when they go on sale and that emotion is what leads them to buy high and sell low...but I digress. Let's close up the point on mutual fund past performance. To wrap this up, I want to relate a story from long ago.

Back in 1963 a mutual fund called Magellan was created by Fidelity Investments. In 1977, the fund changed managers and a fellow by the name of Peter Lynch took the reins of the $20 million portfolio. Lynch had a pretty good track record and sales of the fund exploded. By the time Lynch retired in 1990, the Magellan Fund had grown to some $14 billion and had earned for investors an average annual return of more than 29% per year every year during his tenure.

The fund has never been able to repeat that performance since. Too bad for the investor that bought in the day the next guy took over as manager.

The idea that buying into specific sector funds because one expects them to be "hot" and then selling out of them when they're "not" is every bit the fool's errand that market timing is. There is plenty enough evidence to show that it's a bad idea to invest in something simply because of how it performed in the recent past. Evaluating an investment by looking backward instead of forward is akin to staring into the rear-view mirror as you accelerate onto a freeway onramp. That's not such a great idea.

So What Should You Do?

Much of what we do in our practice is focused on helping people plan for the future. The reality is that the future is a lot more important to the performance of an investment – or an investment strategy for that matter – than is the past.

While we look at data compiled over many years to help us quantify expectations, we really don't use the numbers as a predictor of what may happen in the future. But, as is the case with every research-based decision, you have to start somewhere. And, generally, all data comes from things that have already happened. We use the data to help our clients reach reasonable conclusions about their expectations. Those expectations include the probability of investment returns and risks over long periods of time going out into the future. It may not be perfect, but it works better than anything else we've seen.

Our philosophy is that our clients' investment portfolios should be viewed as the fuel that will power their future lifestyles. As such, we counsel them to have a long-term perspective. But, we also counsel them to view their future lifestyles and their current assets introspectively. Their future lifestyle is unique to them. As such, their investment strategy should likewise be unique to them. What makes sense for one person may not be right for someone else. More importantly, something that works for someone else might not be appropriate for them.

The Bottom Line

Investors should avoid fads, gimmicks, fashions, and trends in the investment world. The more complicated or sexy an investment is, the more likely it is to fail at meeting its stated objective. But, the more complicated or sexy an investment is also makes it more appealing. It can be difficult for people to filter out all of the noise associated with new-fangled and whiz-bangy investment vehicles.

It is also important to realize that owning the next big thing is not necessary to achieving ample investment returns. Beating the market should not be a prerequisite that determines whether or not you can achieve your lifestyle and consumption goals.

Investors should have realistic expectations about their objectives given their current resources, expected future accumulation of resources, and a reasonable expectation of future investment returns. And, it would be a good idea to heed the advice of the late Walt Disney:

"Times and conditions change so rapidly that we must keep our aim constantly focused on the future."

CHAPTER 4

ENGINEER BILL & THE MONEY MONSTER

Wild, Sexy, Hot

A COUPLE OF years ago we were introduced to a new client named Bill. Bill is an engineer at a local tech company. He makes a good living. He's single and is a pretty accomplished amateur athlete, which one would assume by looking at him. Bill is all of fifty-three years old. He's a dashing character, about six-feet-tall; rugged, a bit shy, and as meticulous as a house cat. He is conscientiously saving for retirement…which he'll likely spend traveling to far-off places to compete in triathlons.

When we first met Bill, he told us that he would like to be in a position where he could retire at age sixty-five, but wasn't sure if he could. He was resigned to the notion that he may have to work well into his seventies.

"Heck," he would joke, "if Betty White can still go into work every day, I don't see any reason why I can't keep doing what I'm doing for a couple more decades."

The genesis of Bill's work comment was the result of his recent investment experience. On that first meeting he explained that the last decade had been an exhausting ordeal because he had been following the misguided advice of a "screeching, bald-headed madman".

Oddly, Bill had no financial advisor during all that time. Instead he had been an avid follower of a brash stock-picker who both entertained and offered "sage" investment advice on an hour-long television program on a cable network. Bill religiously followed (and sadly invested in) the stock picks of the vociferous host as if he had been following the prophecies of a zealot. And then one day, he had an epiphany.

As it turns out, Bill would have fared a lot better if he had simply invested in the S&P 500 over that same ten-year period. The investment performance of the stock-picker's ideas provided an average annual return that was more than 3% worse than that of the unmanaged index.[2] And, that doesn't take into consideration the commissions that Bill paid to buy and sell those investment gems, those pearls of the guru's wisdom.

Why, we asked, had he been taking investment advice from the host of a television program for so many years?

"Well," Bill told us, "he's on TV. He must be legit, right?"

Wrong!

Let me put this into context. This real-life money monster is a brash TV star who will occasionally dress up in kooky costumes and parade around the stage clanging a cowbell. Sometimes he'll throw a chair to make a point. And, other times he'll scream into the camera like a deranged character out of the 1976 movie Network. So, while the guy is indeed on TV, and is entertaining, I don't think he passes the test as a legitimate investment advisor.

Nevertheless, people accept the idea that only an authority could be on the boob-tube. Television creates a kind of cognitive legitimacy wherein the viewer takes for granted whatever the commentator says. There's no skepticism. Unfortunately, television viewers generally don't make a distinction between investment news, entertainment, and

2 Hartley, Jonathan S. and Olson, Matthew, Jim Cramer's 'Mad Money' Charitable Trust Performance and Factor Attribution (May 12, 2016) using data from 2005 to 2015.

opinion. The result is that they are inclined to buy into the "expert's" advice on face value without questioning its validity.

Bill even said to us in that first meeting that he was more inclined to accept the information coming from the clown on the television than he would have been if the exact same recommendation had come from a licensed or credentialed financial advisor. He said it seemed unbiased.

So, Bill did himself a disservice in two ways. First, he was making investment decisions that affected his retirement based on the guesswork of a guy whose stock picks couldn't match the performance of the S&P 500. And, he accepted the advice as if it was tailored for him, which obviously it wasn't.

The value that a licensed or credentialed financial professional brings to the client/advisor relationship comes from that professional's ability to ask the client questions and develop a plan that can be discussed in real time over time to make sure that it is tailored to the client's current situation and is flexible enough so that it can evolve as circumstances in the client's life change. The "advice" these charlatans give out on their radio and television shows is no more genuine or tailored for the audience member who asks for it than are the canned visions you'd get from an online psychic.

In Bill's case, he was taking investment advice from someone who didn't know anything about him. He had no clue what Bill's personal circumstances were. He didn't know what Bill's risk tolerances were. He had no idea what Bill's hopes, goals, wants, or dreams might be. And, he certainly could not have known whether common stocks were even appropriate for Bill. Those are the things a financial advisor needs to know before ever designing a client's investment plan.

And, that's the key ingredient that's missing when one takes the investment advice lauded by some knucklehead on the radio or television. Those people don't have to be careful, cautious, or conservative with their recommendations. They're not actually advising clients. What they are doing is *entertaining* an audience. That's why those characters need to be bigger than life. They need to be bold, brash, sarcastic, over-the-top, boisterous clowns. That's what makes good television.

Those are the important qualities for a talk-radio host. But, those really aren't the traits you want in your lawyer, accountant, or financial advisor. And, let's not kid ourselves. The people offering financial advice on the TV or radio are entertainers. Don't lose sight of that.

When I was a kid there was one show on television dedicated to reporting on Wall Street and business matters. The name of the program, which still airs on PBS, was the Nightly Business Report. The show, at that time, was hosted by a stuffy old grump named Paul Kangas. Kangas didn't offer advice or pitch stocks. He was no entertainer. He simply read the news from behind a desk. The show was an insomniac's dream come true. There was little...actually nothing...on TV as boring. Ah, the good old days!

Today there are dozens of money monsters across every form of mass media. They constantly bombard would-be investors with all manner of financial baloney. They appear on the three cable business networks, broadcast television, and various syndicated radio networks; all of which broadcast their fodder twenty-four hours every day. Cumulatively, that's a lot of hours of content. There is more financial content available every day than there are eyes and ears to see or hear it. The network that attracts the most of those eyes and ears can charge the most money to advertisers. The best way to attract those viewers and listeners is to appeal to their most prurient financial interest: making lots of money. And, that's why programming dedicated to Wall Street has transmogrified from one sleepy show on public television into a genre that forces down the throats of Americans the notion that investing in the stock market is wild, sexy, and hot!

In the mid-1990s, financial journalist Jane Bryant Quinn coined the phrase ***Investment Pornography*** to describe the salacious manner in which business and investment news was being reported. "You know the stories," she said "the Top Ten Mutual Funds to Buy Now, How to Double Your Money This Year. Personality profiles that read like fan magazines...investment pornography – softcore, not hardcore – but pornography all the same."

Perhaps it was soft in the nineties, but today it's completely hardcore. And, it's not just on the radio and television. It's in newspapers and magazines. And, it's thrown at us in real-time all over the Internet. Investment pornography is inescapable. Its pop-ads clog our computer screens and penny-stock promotions fill our inboxes. It's nearly impossible for even the most pious saver to ignore. The lure is mesmerizing. You want to turn away, but you can't help but look. It's almost naughty. And, Americans gobble this junk up like it was candy!

And, that's how it should be treated. There's nothing wrong with candy. But, most adults know that it shouldn't be the foundation of your diet. The same can be said of investment pornography and the so-called gurus that peddle it. It's entertainment. Entertainment is fun. Don't take it seriously. And, whatever you do, certainly don't follow it as if it were actually sound investment advice!

Gurus Gone Wild

Unfortunately, investment gurus are not restricted to television and radio. They're everywhere. They're on the Internet, in investment newspapers and magazines. And, lots of them publish their own newsletters; both physical and electronic. But, don't be fooled! These gurus don't exist to help you make money. It's not about you getting rich. It's about them getting rich!

They're there to either sell you a subscription or count your eyeballs as part of an audience that they sell to advertisers. That's how they make their money. Because the investment ideas and stock picks they offer to you are not the source of their revenue, they don't have to be any good. It's not as if they won't be paid if their stock picks lose value. They've already got your money. But, no matter what media outlets are the "gurus" behind these things, all have one remarkable thing in common.

They are all just guessing! Market prognosticators don't know any more than you or I know about the market or the direction of a given stock over a given period of time. The so-called gurus aren't right even 50% of the time. You could almost do better flipping a coin.

Take a look at the table below. According to the Hulbert Investment Digest, a company that tracks the performance of investment advisory newsletters, the coin toss appears to actually be the safer bet. The average return of two-thirds of the newsletters that have been in business for thirty years can't match the performance of the Vanguard 500 Index Fund. The Vanguard 500 Index Fund was created back in 1975 and was the first unmanaged (passive) investment vehicle designed to track the performance of the S&P 500.

30-Year Performance Through April 30, 2017		
Newsletter	**Portfolio**	**Return**
PaulMerriman.com	**Newsletter Equity Portfolio Average**	**6.84**
Bob Brinker's Marketimer	**Newsletter Equity Portfolio Average**	**9.89**
NoLoad FundX	**Newsletter Average**	**10.39**
Investment Quality Trends	**Newsletter Average**	**11.11**
Vanguard 500 Index Fund		**11.31**
The Investment Reporter	**Newsletter Average**	**11.97**
The Prudent Speculator	**Newsletter Average**	**12.21**

Source: HulbertRatings.com/30-Year-Scorecard

As the table above points out, the average returns of the newsletters listed above in the light gray field didn't beat the average return of the S&P 500 over that thirty-year period. The ones in darker gray did. The two shown above that provided positive incremental return over the S&P 500 (the Vanguard index fund) did so only modestly. And, quite frankly, that positive variance would completely disappear after brokerage fees and commissions were taken into consideration. Hulbert points out something more interesting than the results above, however.

According to Hulbert's "Sentiment Indices"[3], in general, newsletters tend to be "most bullish at or near market tops and most bearish at or near bottoms". Does that sound to you like the prescient wisdom of an enlightened expert? To me it sounds like the result you'd get after polling thirty drunks at a Boston Bruins game.

The important point to remember here is that newsletter publishers don't manage money for clients. They don't have to be right. They can boast all they want about achieving spectacular investment returns

3 www.hulbertratings.com/about

– even if those returns are not independently verified – because they aren't in the (regulated) investment advisory business. They are in the opinion publishing business. And, the folks behind most newsletters don't have any special vision of the market. So, you shouldn't expect that their stock picks are going to perform any better than the overall market. And, according to the Hulbert Investment Digest, most can't even achieve that benchmark.

Okay. But, what if we looked at the investment returns of folks that actually *are* in the (regulated) investment advisory business? If we reviewed the audited and verified returns of active money managers, would we see different results than the sort shown by the celebrity gurus out there? What if we limited our search to just the super-smart gurus that are well-known for their prowess at managing other people's money? Not all of them; just the really famous ones. Surely their investment results would have to beat the S&P 500, right?

Wrong!

Before we look, let's refine our search of investment gurus. After all, we can't look at the investment performance of every schlub out there that gives any kind of investment advice. We're only looking for the cream of the crop, the top of the heap, the real know-it-alls, the experts, the leading lights, the pundits, masters, specialists, authorities, and bona fide whiz kids of the investment management business. We're only going to be looking at the folks who have everything necessary to beat the market; the brains, the brawn, the bravura, and lots of other people's money! And, to find these leaders in the field, we have to go to the source.

Thank goodness there actually is a dedicated repository that catalogs information about the world's greatest "investment gurus". Seriously, you can't make this stuff up! It's on the Internet, of course.

The site is called GuruFocus, and they actually maintain a running scoreboard of investment advisor returns. That's where the data in the table below comes from. And, as in the previous table showing the performance of the newsletters, the folks in light gray are the ones that didn't beat the index. The ones in dark gray are the few that did.

10-Year Performance Through April 30, 2017					
Manager	Fund Type	Return	Manager	Fund Type	Return
Ronald Muhlenkamp	Mutual Fund	(0.20)	Ruane Cunniff	Mutual Fund	6.00
Arnold Van Den Berg	Mutual Fund	1.10	NWQ Managers	Mutual Fund	6.00
Third Avenue Management	Mutual Fund	2.10	Ron Baron	Mutual Fund	6.10
Charles Brandes	Mutual Fund	2.10	Bruce Berkowitz	Mutual Fund	6.40
Martin Whitman	Mutual Fund	2.20	Robert Bruce	Mutual Fund	6.60
Arnold Schneider	Mutual Fund	2.90	Mario Gabelli	Mutual Fund	6.60
Mason Hawkins	Mutual Fund	3.20	First Eagle Investment	Mutual Fund	6.80
Private Capital	Hedge Fund	3.60	Meridian Funds	Mutual Fund	6.90
David Winters	Mutual Fund	3.90	John Rogers	Mutual Fund	7.10
Ken Fisher	Mutual Fund	4.00	Barrow, Hanley, Mewhinney & Strauss	Mutual Fund	7.50
Ken Heebner	Mutual Fund	4.00	John Paulson	Hedge Fund	7.90
David Dreman	Mutual Fund	4.00	Vanguard 500 Index Fund		8.49
Robert Olstein	Mutual Fund	4.20	Mariko Gordon		8.50
HOTCHKIS & WILEY	Mutual Fund	4.30	Bill Nygren	Mutual Fund	8.50
David Einhorn	Hedge Fund	4.50	Warren Buffett	Investment Company	9.40
Wallace Weitz	Mutual Fund	4.50	Yacktman Fund	Mutual Fund	9.40
Leucadia National	Investment Company	4.60	Donald Yacktman	Mutual Fund	9.40
Chris Davis	Mutual Fund	4.60	Yacktman Focused Fund	Mutual Fund	9.80
Keeley Asset Management Corp	Mutual Fund	4.80	Vanguard Health Care Fund	Mutual Fund	10.20
Tweedy Browne	Mutual Fund	4.90	Chuck Akre	Mutual Fund	11.20
FPA Capital Fund	Mutual Fund	5.40	Bill Ackman	Hedge Fund	12.80
T Rowe Price Equity Income Fund	Mutual Fund	5.70	Seth Klarman	Hedge Fund	12.80
Dodge & Cox	Mutual Fund	5.90	Prem Watsa	Investment Company	13.10
Tom Gayner	Investment Company	6.00	David Tepper	Hedge Fund	20.10

Source: GuruFocus.com/Score_Board

And, wouldn't you know it; the coin toss still beats the majority of these money management maharishis. What we see above is that fully 75% of the fund managers studied by GuruFocus couldn't beat the S&P 500 over a ten-year period. The one on the list with the best reported performance is a moot point for mere mortals like you and me. David Tepper, manager of the Appaloosa Management hedge fund has a minimum investment requirement of $5 million.

So, if the money monsters on television and radio, and the investment newsletter writers, and the smartest institutional money managers – gurus all – can't beat the market, how would we advise you about attempting to do it? Well, be patient. I'm going to get there soon enough. First let's explore an important aspect of the financial news mass media and how it affects the typical financial advisor.

Take the Quiz

The Markets Will Go:

A. Up

B. Down

It Will Happen:

A. Today

B. This Week

C. This Month

D. This Year

Some financial advisors seem to be obsessed with daily market movement, as if they're startled by its unpredictability. I often wonder if they sit at their desks staring at the blinking red and green lights on their workstations consciously wondering, "Oh my, what's happening"? And, then returning the next morning only to see the same phenomenon and ask, "Why is this happening again"?

My position is that advisors who spend time trying to figure out why the market is behaving as it is would be better served by helping clients understand why it doesn't matter. Nevertheless, there are lots of financial advisors that spend inordinate amounts of time glancing back and forth between their workstations and the televisions in their offices that are tuned to one of the three cable business networks. I suspect that part of the reason for this is a sincere desire to explain to clients why the market is up or down on any given day. Perhaps they think that they'll be perceived as unknowledgeable (or unnecessary) if they admit that they don't know. So, they keep the television on in order to mimic what the money monsters are saying in an effort to appear smart.

Now, I'm sure this next statement is not going to come across to you as a revelation. But, markets fluctuate ***EVERY*** day! And, these fluctuations are out of anyone's control. The smartest institutional investment managers, most experienced floor traders, and most seasoned industry veterans get lessons in humility nearly every day on Wall Street. And, not one of them can, at the end of any given day explain exactly why the market went up or down.

There are lots of reasons. So many, in fact, that dozens of books have been written on the subject. The fact that there are "reasons" that markets move doesn't mean that any one of them is relevant! Understanding the key underlying cause of today's stock market action will not increase your long-term investment performance. What takes place on the floor of the New York Stock Exchange today is immaterial. It will not change the outcome of a well-thought-out, durable investment plan. The same can be said about interest rates and the folly of worrying about how they might change in the foreseeable future.

In 2009, the Wall Street Journal polled fifty of the most talented economic forecasters in the investment business about their predictions for interest rates one year into the future. Not one of their predictions was right. None of them accurately called the direction of rates; therefore, none of them came anywhere close to correctly guessing the actual rate. There is a chance that some of their clients made investment decisions based on those predictions. Yikes! Here's my point.

Whatever the change in interest rates will be a year from now – or even two years from now – just doesn't matter. Making investment decisions based on a prediction is a fool's errand. Because, as with short-term fluctuations in stock prices, changes in interest rates will not change the outcome of a well-thought-out, durable investment plan. And, here's where I want to connect the dots between the hyperbole of the financial news mass media, its obsession with trying to explain current market moves (and predicting future moves), and the average investment advisor.

Financial advisors that pay too close attention to the financial news mass media (and I suspect that they watch more of that programing than the average investor does) are likely to cognitively legitimize the persistent predictions they hear. The more exposure, the more inclined some advisors are to act on news. Market news can challenge even the most disciplined investor. That's when having an advisor that divorces himself or herself from that noise can be of great value. If your advisor is inclined to take at face value that which is being blasted over the airwaves, then you run the risk of having your investment plan upended by him or her reacting to some short-term event.

Advisors are people too. They can also fall prey to the influence of the money monsters and celebrity investment gurus. So, as a cautionary note, beware of the advisory firm that plays market news while you are on hold or has a TV tuned to one of the big financial networks in the lobby of the office. Remember what Jane Bryant Quinn said. That stuff is tempting to watch and is hugely entertaining. And, that's the whole point! It's entertainment. That's why you should never act on it!

So What Should You Do?

The main lesson we can take away from engineer Bill's story and our discussion about the investment returns of the various gurus is quite straightforward: even the smartest people on Wall Street can't beat the market. Of course, I need to explain this by telling a story about another client of ours.

One of our very first clients is a former school teacher named Martha. The best way to describe Martha is that she is the female version of a cross between the Extra-Terrestrial in the movie E.T. and Yoda from the Star Wars movies. She is more of a cuddly teddy bear than a person and is just so adorable that you want to hug her every time you see her. Martha is a small lady and a bit hunched over. She is a beautiful, magical person and has more wrinkles than a Shar Pei. Her eyes are so big and bright and full of life that you get the sense that she can see into your soul.

Clearly, we know that she can see. She once came into the office with some material that we sent out to her. She laid the piece of paper in front of me. Emblazoned in the middle of one of the paragraphs was a big circle drawn with a thick red marker. She had found a typo. Old teachers never retire.

The next time Martha came in, I cringed. She had something in her hand and I feared she had found another misspelling in some correspondence. Luckily, she was clutching a copy of Kiplinger's newsletter and not something I had written. On this visit Martha was as excited as I had ever seen her.

"We must look into this!" Martha declared as she placed the magazine on the conference room table.

The article she referenced was describing an investment that had experienced a performance history that she thought had been good over the last ten years. Oh boy, she thought she had discovered a hidden treasure! When she showed me the article, it was about the Vanguard S&P 500 Index ETF, the closed-end exchange-traded fund version of John Bogle's very first index fund! This is the same fund that I used above to compare the investment returns of the newsletter gurus and the investment management gurus. It is a proxy for the S&P 500. No magic here, just long-term passive investing.

In the first chapter, I introduced our use of Financial Planning and Strategic Asset Allocation to inform the unique investment plans we create for each client. No two are ever the exact same. The one element that is the same for absolutely all of our clients is our firm belief that active investment management does not work over the long-term.

At this point, defining the difference between active investment management and passive investment management is important. Here is how William F. Sharpe, PhD defines the difference. This is an excerpt from his essay The Arithmetic of Active Management[4]

> "A passive investor always holds every security from the market, with each represented in the same manner as in the market.
>
> An active investor…usually act[s] on perceptions of mispricing, and because such misperceptions change relatively frequently, such managers tend to trade fairly frequently – hence the term 'active.'"

4 The Financial Analysts' Journal Vol. 47, No. 1, January/February 1991. pp. 7-9. Copyright, 1991, Association for Investment Management and Research, Charlottesville, VA.

Bill Sharpe teaches Finance at Stanford University's Graduate School of Business. He won the 1990 Nobel Prize in Economics and is the creator of the Sharpe Ratio, an indicator of risk-adjusted investment rate of return. He's a pretty smart guy.

What Sharpe says (in plain English) is that a passive investor buys and holds the market and makes no changes. An active investor owns some individual stocks and rejects other individual stocks from that same market and that selection of stocks will change over time. So, for example, if the market is the S&P 500, then a passive investor would own all 500 stocks in the index and would own them in the exact same proportion as they are represented in the index. The active investor would own far fewer than all 500 stocks and the ones he or she did own would not be in the same proportion as they are represented in the index. And, he or she wouldn't own them for long periods of time.

Now consider for a moment that there are lots of different "markets". There are stock markets, bond markets, money markets, domestic and foreign markets, and markets for small stocks, medium stocks, and large stocks. The universe of equity markets is vast.

The whole concept of a "market" is a place (physical or virtual) where buyers and sellers come together to exchange things. In the context of this discussion, those things are shares of stock. The market has zillions of participants simultaneously offering for sale and bidding for purchase the shares of thousands of companies, which are instantaneously bought and sold in real time at the speed of light.

The Efficient Market Hypothesis, tells us that markets are pretty good at accurately determining price. The mechanism for this is those zillions of bidders and offerors instantaneously determining prices by agreeing to zillions of transactions every single day the market is open. The prices at which all of these transactions are exchanged take into account all known information about everything relevant to every share traded in that market. The result is that the market is accurate.

The very popular practice of active investment management is based on the belief that one lone genius picking just some stocks and not others from the vast universe of those available can achieve higher investment returns than the zillions of other participants in the market. The notion is that this one stock-picking mastermind knows more than everyone else. It then follows that this brilliance is not manifest in one single event. It is a regularly occurring phenomenon. It assumes that this savant has this degree of clairvoyance not just once when he or she originally buys said stock, but over and over and over again. And, this telepathic gift exists not just when he or she buys something that is "undervalued", but also when he or she sells something that is "overvalued".

This is what is happening when the money monster, the newsletter writer, or the investment management guru announce their latest "hot stock pick" on TV. The best way to explain the fallacy of this philosophy is to compare it to the practice of passive investment management. For discussion sake, I'll use the S&P 500 index as our "market".

At the inception of our passive investment fund, our manager buys all 500 stocks in the exact proportion as they are represented in the S&P index. There are some commissions due on these purchases and then there are other fees and expenses related to running the business of watching those 500 stocks over time. Every now and then, the components of the S&P 500 change. On average, twenty-two companies get replaced each year. So, the passive manager incurs some costs to make those changes. That's it.

The active manager is going to incur the same costs of running the business (rent, salaries, utilities, etc.) as is our manager. So, initially, we're on par with each other. But, the virtuoso at the active fund is constantly looking for a mismatch between market prices and inherent value in all 500 companies. So, he or she is going to spend some money that we don't have to spend in order to have a research analyst on staff to look for bargains to buy. We don't have that expense, because we won't buy or sell anything unless there is a change to some component of the index. The active manager now has a cost of doing business that puts him or her at a disadvantage to us. But, wait; there's more.

The more value disparity that research analyst finds, the more often that active manager is going to discover his or her latest hot stock pick.

To get that stock into the portfolio, the active manager is going to have to pay a commission to own it. He or she is also going to have to pay a separate commission to sell the thing they now realize is a dog to make room for that new high-investment-return-generating magic bullet. This is because the fund won't have any cash on hand. After all, clients don't pay these gurus to hold zero-return-generating cash. They expect them to be fully invested in the market. So, again, the cost of doing business just keeps getting bigger for the active manager. This is going to eat into his or her total return. So, those hot stock picks better be sizzling! If they're not, then the active portfolio's return might fall short of the overall market. And, that doesn't take into consideration the risk of what I like to call the tide.

Folks on Wall Street have a cute saying that a rising tide lifts all boats. It means that if the market rises, all stocks will benefit. On the contrary, if the market declines, then all stocks will suffer. This presents a big risk to the active investment manager vis-à-vis the passive manager.

The reason for this is that there are only 500 stocks in the market from which to choose. The passive manager owns them all. But, the active manager doesn't. So, the ones the active manager does own represent a bigger proportion of his or her portfolio than they do for the passive manager. If the market declines, the passive manager's returns will match the market...because the portfolio is the market. The active manager's portfolio will decline more than the market because he or she has taken bigger bets on fewer stocks.

And, all of these factors explain why the money monster, the newsletter publisher, and the gifted investment manager don't consistently "beat the market".

The Bottom Line

No matter what work goes into determining the gurus' latest hot stock picks, the reality is that their results are statistically no more impressive than one would achieve by tossing a dart at the stock listing from a newspaper.

That's why our investment approach uses a buy and hold portfolio designed to meet each person's individual risk tolerance. If you find that the markets are making you unable to sleep at night, reduce the risk but don't sell entirely. Stop asking your advisor for a reason the market is moving up or down. That's what markets do! And, heed the advice of Warren Buffett, Chairman of Berkshire Hathaway:

"Huge institutional investors, viewed as a group, have long underperformed the unsophisticated index-fund investor who simply sits tight for decades. A major reason has been fees: Many institutions pay substantial sums to consultants who, in turn, recommend high-fee managers. And that is a fool's game."

CHAPTER 5

MR. ROGERS' NEIGHBORHOOD

Home Sweet Home...Until It's Broken

It was a sad day when we first met Ana Platypus. She came in not long after her divorce from Dr. Bill Platypus was finalized. Ana was in desperate need of financial planning help. The settlement she received when the thirty-five-year marriage ended didn't leave her with much. Bill kept his pension and the 401 (k) he had established and Ana ended up with some personal property and the couple's house. The items of personal property had more sentimental value than actual worth. While the house was fully paid for, its ongoing maintenance expenses were a drain on Ana's finances. For all intents and purposes, Ana was destitute. Her salary as an office manager was barely enough to cover her living expenses. There wasn't anything left over to save. And, she had no investable assets to create retirement income for her after she stopped working.

Ana had been through a great deal emotionally and it had clearly taken a toll on her. Her countenance was perpetually sullen. Ana's hazel eyes appeared gray to us when we first met her. On that original encounter, gray seemed to be the best descriptor of everything about her. She looked a lot older than her sixty-two years would otherwise have suggested.

Divorce is a tough ordeal to endure, but ultimately, Ana got through it okay. I'll go into more detail on that later. First, I want to introduce another client: Miss Audrey Paulificate. We call her Missy.

Missy is a firecracker. She's a bubbly, young, forty-something, unmarried, and carefree. She might make a good match for Engineer Bill, but we've never suggested it to either of them. Missy was in a similar situation as Ana when she came in for our initial conversation.

Her parents had passed away. Her mom went first, then a few years later, her dad. When her father died, Missy inherited a more-than-modest amount of money, which she used to get out of debt and buy a very nice house. It would actually make a beautiful home to raise a slew of kids with Engineer Bill. I think they'd make a cute couple. Please don't tell them I said that! Here's the issue Missy had when we first met.

She was debt-free, had a huge house, but had very little money saved for retirement. As is the case now, she was gainfully employed as a software systems analyst (see how this match with Bill just makes so much sense), but knew that what she was able to contribute to her 401 (k) wouldn't accumulate to enough to live on in retirement. At the end of the Chapter I'll go into detail about how we helped Missy. In the meantime, I want to discuss the idea of owning a home free and clear.

There is no argument that having a paid-for house in retirement provides security and reduces the amount of income needed to live the rest of your life without worry. Paying off the mortgage on your primary home while still working ***and*** saving for retirement is the optimal solution (notice the emphasis on the word 'and'). Liquid assets are necessary to provide an income stream for most people in retirement. Social security will not be enough to live on. And, for most Americans, corporate pensions are all but nostalgia. It is impossible to retire on nothing but a house. So, sacrificing a future retirement nest egg for the purpose of owning your house free and clear today is ill-advised. This is a place where the prudent use of leverage actually makes sense.

What makes the concept of owning an unencumbered house so attractive anyway? In reality, the reason is more emotional than financial. A 2015 report from Merrill Lynch/Age Wave[5] found that 56% of Focus Group Participants between the ages of 65 and 74 said that the emotional value of their home was more important than its monetary value. For participants aged 75 years and older, the percentage increased to 63%. And, in our firm's experience, it becomes clearer every day that emotional decisions of this type often outweigh financial ones.

This goes far in explaining the reason we have seen far too many people who are what I call, "house poor". They have taken an inheritance or made double payments on their mortgage in an effort to eliminate the debt without adequately providing for retirement savings to fund their lifestyle after they stop working. Sacrificing for a paid-for house can leave you cash-strapped and have a serious impact on the life you've planned in retirement.

Financially, homeownership is akin to a consumable rather than an investment in many parts of the country. Real estate prices do not always go up. Will Rogers had a couple things to say about investments in real estate. The first was based on its scarcity.

"...there was only so much of it and no more, and that they wasn't making any more..."

The old adage suggests that you should put your money in land, because they aren't making any more of it. That may be true, but it doesn't mean that real estate is always a great investment. Rogers' less famous quote on real estate gets to the point of its inherent risk.

"Put it in land, and you can always walk on it. We did, but no buyers would walk on it with us."

Real estate is a great investment only if you can sell it. The longer you have to wait to do that, the less and less great it becomes. But, people will argue that if you have time, then real estate never loses its potential to be a great investment. That might be true if you have unlimited time. But, our lives are finite. As time goes by, the money

5 Home in Retirement: More Freedom, New Choices: A Merrill Lynch Retirement Study conducted in partnership with Age Wave.

you have tied up in a piece of property could be needed for other consumption purposes. If that happens, then those assets do you no good. Because real estate is illiquid, the funds you have tied up in it are completely inaccessible. That's not productive.

To take a line out of the real estate investor's playbook, your money ought to be put to its "highest and best" use. Paying off your mortgage before it is due or buying a home without mortgage financing does not put your money to its highest and best use. Doing either of those things will limit your opportunity to generate future portfolio income. They will also reduce your overall investment diversification. And, broad investment diversification is the hallmark of good retirement planning. Putting all your eggs in one basket is generally a bad idea. It can have disastrous effects if the value of that basket is in decline when you need to sell it.

In the current interest rate climate, the cost of mortgage borrowing is still near historic lows. Owning a home is one of the very few ways average folks can afford to use financial leverage because home loans are secured by the underlying property. So, the decision to use liquid assets to acquire or (extinguish the loan on) an illiquid investment is one to consider very carefully.

The penultimate factor in evaluating whether or not to pay off your mortgage is its tax deductibility. This is the least important factor in the equation and I'll discuss that a little more in Chapter Nine. Nonetheless, taxes are still another thing to think about as you contemplate paying down your mortgage. One last point to consider regarding the notion of prematurely paying off a mortgage is this

There's a goofball on the radio who talks a lot about real estate, investing, and financial freedom. The main message he preaches is that all callers to his show should pay off their mortgages. This genius makes this point about mortgages just about every time his show airs.

His shtick is that he has a unique perspective on borrowing to buy houses. That unique perspective comes from his having amassed a multi-million-dollar net worth before losing everything in bankruptcy by the time he was just twenty-seven. His jaundiced view that debt is dangerous is the toxic byproduct of his own unfortunate experience (as

Warren Buffett aptly said, "When you combine ignorance and leverage, you get some pretty interesting results").

This radio financial-evangelist tells everyone who calls into his show to pay off their mortgage even though he doesn't have the foggiest notion what their unique financial situations might be. This irritates me, not just because he has a one-size-fits-all approach to achieving financial freedom, but because he spews his so-called investment wisdom in between commercials that promote his traveling money-making/get-rich-quick seminars that he claims will make attendees millionaires.

Give me a break!

All of this leads me to a couple important points. The first is that individuals ought to approach the decision of whether or not to use investment leverage only in the context of its compatibility with the other financial decisions they make. I'll explore this first point in the Addendum at the end of the book. The second point I want to make is that real estate doesn't provide comparable investment returns to what can be earned in the stock market. So, why would an individual who is not actively engaged in the real estate business put any more money into it than is necessary to secure financing on his or her primary residence? Let's look at the numbers.

The graph below illustrates how $10,000 would have grown between January 1994 and December 2016 if it had been invested in US Stocks, an index of managed REITs (Real Estate Investment Trusts), and a composite of US Home Prices[6].

---

6 Source for assets classes:

Stocks

AQR US MKT Factor Returns 1972-1992 (AQR Data Sets), Vanguard Total Stock Market Index Fund (VTSMX) 1993 and beyond.

Managed REITs

DFA Real Estate Securities I (DFREX) 1994-1996, Vanguard REIT Index Fund (VGSIX) 1997 and beyond.

Home Prices

S&P Dow Jones Indices LLC, S&P/Case-Shiller U.S. National Home Price Index©.

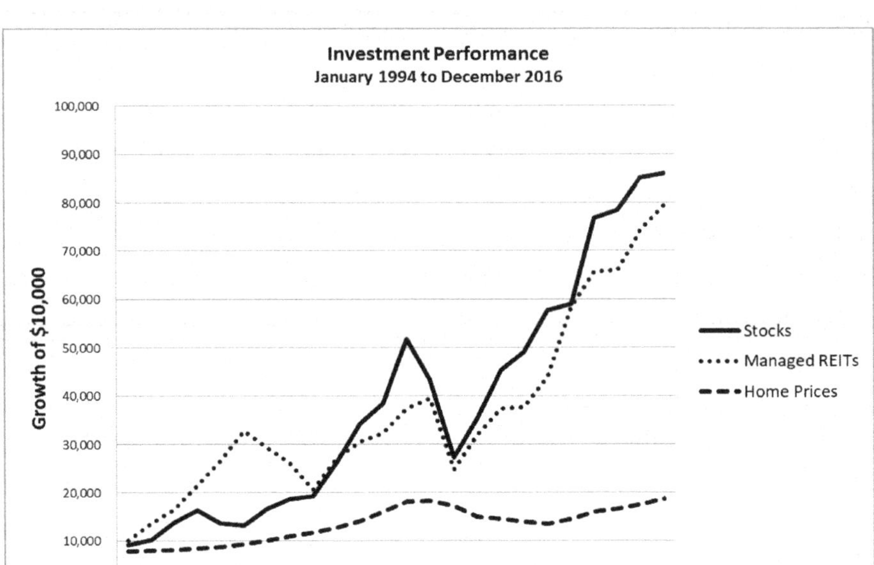

The compound annual growth rate (remember, CAGR) for stocks over the twenty-three-year period represented above was 9.66%. For managed REITS, the CAGR was 9.28%. And, for home prices around the United States, the rate was a miniscule 3.81%. But, that 3.81% is something of a chimera. There is no managed index, mutual fund, or Exchange Traded Fund (ETF) that tracks home prices in the United States. So, the only way you could have actually earned that (terrible) 3.81% would have been if you had all of your money tied up in unencumbered residential real estate. And, that doesn't take into consideration any of the cash expenses you would have incurred to maintain that portfolio of single family homes. Here's the sad part.

The 3.81% represents an average. So, half the homes in America appreciated more rapidly than that compound annual rate. The other half rose in value at an annual rate lower than 3.81%. So, the real estate market in your hometown may not have done as well as the national average. And, that means that unless you really understand your local market (i.e., are in the real estate business) you're taking a crapshoot regarding the long-term appreciation potential of your house.

So what, right? Homeownership is sentimental, not financial, right? Therefore, it doesn't hurt to pay for the home with cash (or to pay off the mortgage early). Those are smart financial decisions, right?

Wrong!

Let's look at an example. We'll assume that you're one of the lucky folks that live in a neighborhood where home prices are rising faster than the national average. Let's say your house will ***really*** smoke that growth rate – your house is going to appreciate 30% faster than 3.81%. That comes to a bit more than 4.5%. And, your home's value is going to appreciate at that rate for the next 20 years. Woo hoo!

Scenario One: No Debt				
	Value of Home	Mortgage	Investment Portfolio	Net Worth
Year One	500,000	0	0	500,000
Year Twenty	1,314,823	0	0	1,314,823

As you can see in the table above, owning your house free and clear more than doubled your money after twenty years. So, having no mortgage looks like a good financial decision. But, what would happen if, instead of paying all cash for that house, you took out a mortgage?

In this next scenario, you borrow 80% of the home's initial value by taking out a 20-year mortgage. With the money left over, you invest in US stocks. Then, you leave that money in the stock market for the same twenty years. Let's assume that your portfolio will generate capital gains along the way and that you're going to use some of the money in your investment portfolio to pay taxes on those gains. Let's also assume that capital gains will be taxed at 20%. This means that your stock portfolio's after-tax investment return will be right around 7.73%.

In the next table we see the effect on your net worth when you borrow money to buy the house and use the money that would have otherwise gone into it to buy stocks.

At the end of twenty years, you will have paid off your $400,000 mortgage. Your home will still have appreciated at 4.5% a year for two decades. But, your investment portfolio will have more than quadrupled in value. These numbers don't include the cost of financing and fees but the general premise remains. By using mortgage financing to purchase the home, your total net worth increases substantially. Now, that's something to get sentimental about!

Scenario Two: 20-Year Mortgage				
	Value of Home	Mortgage	Investment Portfolio	Net Worth
Year One	500,000	(400,000)	400,000	500,000
Year Twenty	1,314,823	0	1,772,686	3,087,509

Big Wigs, Fat Cats, & A Generous Dose of Non-transparency

H.M. Hulamouse has been a client of ours for years. He cleverly refers to himself as Moose, and when I first spoke with him on the phone, I would have sworn that I had been talking to a six-foot-eight former linebacker. Moose has a radio voice, deep throaty, the kind you'd expect to hear on commercials announcing the arrival in town of the Monster Truck Series.

At five-foot-two, he comes in a full four inches shorter than the late Wally Cox; who would have appeared to be a bodybuilder compared to the diminutive Moose. While in appearance he is more mouse than moose, he carries himself like a giant and is one of the most self-confident men I have ever met.

Like most of our clients, Moose has a keen sense of humor. He has innate intelligence, is well-read, and highly analytical; not the traits you'd expect from a guy who never graduated from high school. Moose is a retired civil servant. I'm not exactly sure what he did for the government but it wouldn't surprise me if he was a secret agent during the cold war. In any event, aside from a very good pension, Moose doesn't have a lot of assets. He is comfortable and secure, but certainly not rich.

When Moose engaged our firm as his financial advisor, he had been sitting on cash for a few years but had only just recently fired his former broker. The impetus for the dismissal was what Moose called the last straw. After rebuffing repeated pitches by the broker to get back into the stock market, he was ultimately presented with an "opportunity to make a killing in real estate". Perhaps the broker had given up trying to sell "conventional" products and thought that offering Moose something considerably more complicated and seemingly exclusive would motivate him to part with the contents of his wallet. The great opportunity was a private Real Estate Limited Partnership (RELP) that the broker hissed was, "a great deal reserved only for my best clients". That's when Moose headed for the door.

A private Real Estate Limited Partnership? Seriously?

Private RELPs were all the rage at the big "wirehouse" brokerage firms back in the 1980s. They were part of a bevy of whiz-bang products created to offer clients tax advantages and not much more. Most of the money in these schemes is made by the creators of the partnership. Some of the common themes of these limited partnerships were oil & gas exploration deals, low-income housing deals, equipment lease finance deals, etc. I thought these things had died forever back in the '80s, but apparently not. I hadn't seen a subscription agreement for one since then. The one presented to Moose offered a land deal somewhere in Nevada.

Like all private partnerships, this particular RELP offered the promise of huge investment returns. That's why these things are attractive to investors. But, they aren't always what they seem. As far as investments go, they can be a bit opaque. Here's how they work.

A general partner (typically a separate operating company rather than a live person) creates a company on paper. It finds an underwriter/distributor like Moose's old brokerage firm, which raises money so that the partnership can actually conduct whatever business it's in. The underwriter/distributor pitches the deal to its clients selling them limited partnership interests. They cleverly tell the unwitting stooges that become limited partners that the term limited partner actually means limited risk, which is sort of true. They also, sort-of-correctly, say that the general partner assumes most of the risk in the deal. What they don't typically say during the sales pitch is buried in a huge subscription disclosure document that is written by some wildly expensive Wall Street law firm that composes the prose in an arcane and convoluted form of English that only a Harvard Law School professor could translate.

The disclosure document tells the limited partner that his investment is limited because he or she has no control over how the partnership is managed. It also explains that his or her risk is limited to just the money he or she invests. Gee. That doesn't sound too bad, does it? You have no say in the business but can lose 100% of what you put into the deal. Yikes!

The disclosure document also says that the underwriter/distributor will collect a fee for the hard work they do suckering you into the deal. That fee can be upwards of 8% to 16% of your initial investment. The document also says that the general partner will run the business and take a big fat fee for that.

If all of that wasn't enticing enough, the disclosure document goes on to say that once an investor buys in, it is almost impossible to get out. Limited partnerships don't have a liquid secondary market (like common stocks do). It can take months, if not years, to sell your interest. And, in most cases, the only buyer will be the general partner who will set the price paid to you. That price will back out (or recapture) any income you received during the time you were a partner. That means that you'll have to give back the vast majority of whatever "huge investment returns" you enjoyed during the time you owned the partnership. What's worse is that you really won't have any way of determining whether or not the price the general partner offers you is even remotely fair.

The reason for this is that you may not have access to any of the company's financial statements. If you do, they may not be accurate or complete. This is because these things are private and don't have the same type of reporting requirements that public companies do.

Private Real Estate Limited Partnerships impress me as being formed mostly for the benefit of the sponsors (typically the general partner) not the investor. Their success or failure depends on the quality of the management (the general partner) and the viability of the properties in the partnership. In many cases those properties would have previously been owned by the general partner, who likely enjoyed a huge gain on their sale to the new RELP. That would typically be disclosed in the subscription document, but you can be pretty confident that discussion of it would not be very transparent. These things are typically a murky mess.

RELPs qualify for advantageous tax treatment because they are diminishing assets. By the time the partnership terminates (these things don't last forever), you will have received all of your initial investment. You will have received it as part of the regular payments the partnership pays out to you. In other words, a portion of the income you receive from the partnership is actually a return of your own money. So, the actual rate of return on these types of investments is often far less than promised.

Another unattractive aspect of RELPs is their very structure. Partnerships are pass-through entities. That means that they are not taxed on their earnings. You are. When the partnership files its tax return, it sends you a statement showing your share of the company's earnings. This statement is called a K-1. If the partnership has lots of limited partners it can take months for them to prepare all those K-1s. It is not uncommon for limited partners to receive those statements many months after April 15th. That means that owners of these investments typically have to file extensions on their tax returns, which can create added costs. And, waiting months for a K-1 is generally a nuisance. Now, here's the part about these things that makes them generally unsuitable for most investors and why the one pitched to Moose was absolutely inappropriate for him.

Most RELPs require that limited partners be accredited investors. An accredited investor is a person that meets specifically-defined criteria based on income, net worth, and investment experience. This status is required for a person to make high-risk investments in things like hedge funds, RELPs, or venture capital funds. Accredited investors are folks that have a net worth of at least $1 million (not including their primary residences); or, people whose income for the previous two years has been $200,000 or more. Accredited investors must also have a level of investment experience and sophistication extensive enough for them to be able to understand the risks of these kinds of "deals". While Moose is one smart cookie, he definitely does not meet the other accredited-investor criteria.

The Business of Managed Real Estate Investment Trusts

Real Estate Investment Trust sounds scary. Its acronym, REIT, is reminiscent of RELP. So, it must be just as bad an investment idea, right? Actually, that's not the case. I am including this section on REITs only for the purpose of distinguishing them from RELPs.

Publicly-traded Real Estate Investment Trusts (REITs) differ from RELPs in a number of important ways. The first is that the ones that are available to most investors are publicly traded, just like common stocks. This means that they are very liquid. If you need to get out of the REIT, you can sell it and have your money in two days. Most publicly-traded REITs are listed on major exchanges. As a result, they are subject to the same reporting and disclosure rules that common stocks are. This means operating and financial information is readily available and totally transparent.

By law, REITs have to be formed as corporations. So, they pay the taxes and you avoid the often-delayed K-1. Also, by law, a REIT has to pay out to its shareholders ninety percent of all of its earnings. That translates into big fat dividend yields.

REITs offer investors a way to include a diversified real estate component into their long-term asset allocation. They are divided into two types of structures: equity REITs; and, mortgage REITs. Equity REITs manage a portfolio of real estate. Mortgage REITs manage a portfolio of debt secured by real estate. But, this is not the only diversification that REITs can provide.

Equity REITs give investors the ability to diversify among several different classes of real estate. There are REITs that own only apartment buildings. Some manage portfolios made up exclusively of downtown high-rise office buildings in major cities across the country. Some do the same thing regionally. There are others that specialize in retail properties. And, still others that only own medical centers and hospitals. So, REITs are a lot like mutual funds.

One last benefit that REITs can bring to a diversified portfolio of stocks and bonds is that, in general, they have a low correlation to either asset class. In other words, those three markets (the stock market, the bond market, and the real estate market) don't rise and fall in tandem. This means that during periods of market volatility, the inclusion of REITs in an already well-diversified portfolio can help to further reduce the portfolio's standard deviation – a measure of the portfolio's risk.

So What Should You Do?

Every one of our firm's clients owns a home. Some of them own more than one. Of our clients that own just one home, some have a mortgage on that house; others own the house free and clear. Our clients who own more than one home are all over the board. Some have a mortgage on just one of the houses. Some have a mortgage on two or more of them. Some have a mortgage on all of them. Others don't have a mortgage on any. The common thread weaving through absolutely every client's situation is that the decision to use leverage or not is based on a specific, uniquely-tailored plan that addresses each client's individual situation.

We are completely neutral about the use of mortgage debt – or any financial leverage for that matter. The key determinant of whether or not a client should borrow to make an investment is specific to that client. We don't love or hate debt. We recommend it when it makes sense and discourage it when it does not.

In Ana's case, borrowing against her house to free up cash to fund her living expenses would not have made sense. It would have saddled her with debt service payments and have added to her already tenuous cash flow situation. Likewise, for Ana, a reverse mortgage was an unacceptable option.

A reverse mortgage is a loan secured by the value of the borrower's home. The cash that is "taken out" of the home can be used for any purpose. In Ana's case, she could have used the money to finance her living expenses. A reverse mortgage differs from both a conventional mortgage and a home equity line of credit in that the loan does not come due to be paid off – and in fact requires no payment of principal and interest – until the borrower either moves out, sells the home, or passes away. For Ana, a reverse mortgage would not have helped her meet the continuing high-maintenance expenses on the house.

Ana's adult children were financially secure and as a result, their financial well-being did not play a part in the planning decision she ultimately made (with our guidance, of course). And, the decision Ana made was the most conservative and straightforward one available to her. She downsized.

She sold the house and used a portion of the proceeds to buy a smaller home in a retirement community. This drastically reduced her living expenses. The sale of the old family home freed up enough cash to both make a meaningful down payment on her new bungalow and set aside an investment nest egg that she could draw from in the future if she ever "retired" from the office manager job that she truly loves.

The new community she lives in is populated with singles and couples her own age and she has a very active social life. The last time Ana came into the office she was cheery and bright and several pounds lighter than she had been when we first met. Her demeanor had changed dramatically and she seriously looked ten years younger.

Missy was faced with similar options as Ana. Her decision was likewise conservative and straightforward. For Missy, the most appropriate course of action was to borrow against her dream home and use the proceeds to fund an investment portfolio, the asset allocation of which was consistent with her long-term goals and risk tolerances.

The fact that Missy makes enough money to fund her lifestyle, sock a few bucks away in the company 401(k), and service her one and only debt (her mortgage) is as I mentioned early in the chapter...the optimal solution. She is still working, paying off the mortgage on her primary residence, ***and*** saving for retirement. The fact that she has an additional cushion in the investment portfolio we helped her create offers her additional peace of mind.

At first Missy was reluctant borrow against her house. The idea of owning it free and clear appealed to her on a deeply emotional level. The financial modeling we performed for Missy showed her only two other options; sell the house when she reached age sixty-five (her desired retirement age); or, postpone retirement indefinitely.

Homeownership is a complex financial planning concept. Buying a house is typically the biggest financial decision people make. And, while there are certainly financial benefits that come from homeownership, buying a house is different from acquiring any other asset. There's a lot of "feel" that goes into the decision. So, after questions about the neighborhood, the school district, the number of baths, and the size of the master bedroom are long answered, it is necessary to look at your house as if it really were just an investment. The financial planning questions we have our clients consider are these.

1. Is the house I currently live in too large for my needs in retirement?
2. Do I want to live in this community for the rest of my life?
3. Can I afford this in retirement?
4. How will my emotional attachment to the house change if the kids and grandchildren move across the country?
5. What is my tax situation in retirement?
6. Is my house a good investment?

Asking these questions will help in understanding the purpose and utility of a home. It will ultimately bring clarity to the asset and enable the right decision to be made.

The Bottom Line

Real estate is one of those easy, tricky assets. It's easy in that it's local and you can touch it and feel it. You know your neighborhood and the town in which you live. So, you have an innate sense of the value of the homes on your street and the buildings that house the businesses a few blocks away. It's tricky because most people think that's all you need to be able to make money in it. But, real estate is trickier than that.

Owning income property is not a passive endeavor the way owning an investment portfolio of stocks and bonds is. You never get a call in the middle of the night about a leaky toilet from the CEO of one of the companies that you own in your stock portfolio. You never have to fix the roof or repaint any of the stocks you own. That's not the case with real estate. You need to be in that business to make money at it.

So, unless you are in that business, our advice would be to use REITs to add the asset class to a diversified portfolio. Avoid fancy, new-fangled, whiz-bang schemes like private real estate limited partnerships.

Remember that the most important aspects of homeownership are that a house provides a warm, loving place to raise a family and also offers a nifty tax deduction while you're working. And, while it can augment your net worth in retirement, our advice would mirror what Robert Kiyosaki said in his 1997 book, Rich Dad, Poor Dad:

"Your home is not an asset."

CHAPTER 6

GOLDFINGER & THE RESTAURATEUR

The Zombie Apocalypse

GREG FROST CAN only be described as a surfer dude. Born in Huntington Beach with salt water in his veins, the lanky blonde is the poster child for laid-back Southern California living. His hair never seems to be combed, yet never appears to be unkempt; as if it falls into place as naturally as a wave breaks in shallow water. Greg rides his beach cruiser bike to work every morning unless it rains. On those days he drives his 1950 Plymouth Woodie station wagon. Greg is as mellow as the sea is deep. He's a younger, better-looking version of Gordon Ramsey. And, coincidentally, he is also a restaurateur.

The former General Manager at a national restaurant chain left the corporate world to pursue the American Dream and open a small Mexican grill he owns with his wife Miranda, whom everyone calls Mimi. Now, I am not a restaurant owner and never have been, but I expect that the business is every bit as hectic and stressful as is depicted on those reality television shows that pit aspiring young chefs in competition with one another for a chance at working for Gordon Ramsey.

Yet, no matter how busy their grill seems to get, I have never seen Greg lose his cool. The most excited I have ever seen him was the day he got a call from Auric Fröbe.

"Do we have any gold in my portfolio?" Greg asked after Fröbe's call.

"Do you mean exposure to gold?"

"No. Physical gold. Do we own any physical gold?"

"No, Greg you don't own any physical gold. But, your portfolio is well diversified and actually includes exposure to a number of commodities. Why?"

Greg said that Fröbe, a gold merchant on the east coast, had called to sell him some bullion. Fröbe explained to Greg that owning gold outright was the only way to protect his wealth. He went on to tell him that in the event of a major global crisis, gold would be the only safe haven; that all paper assets would be worthless. And, this actually concerned him.

Okay, it's time for a reality check.

Human nature being what it is will most certainly put the global financial system into a position one day in the future where things will get a bit unnerving. That's not a prediction. It's just a statement of the obvious. Financial markets sometimes get overheated. The next time that happens, the financial media will cleverly dub the event "the whatever-the-catalyst-is crisis". It will scare the life out of lots of otherwise cool-headed investors, sending them into a panic and to the exit.

Now, you don't have to look back very far to see the last one of these things. Not much more than a decade ago the world's financial system was reeling in turmoil when the real estate bubble burst. It was a difficult time to be sure. But, it wasn't the end of the world. And, it wasn't an uncommon event.

There have been literally scores of international financial panics over the last 200 years; lots more prior to that too. And, today there is an abundance of doomsayers on both sides of the political aisle predicting the end of the world in a specific way that fits their unique distorted agenda. The common thread is their insistence that there will be a really big financial collapse somewhere in your lifetime. Those predictions all say that the next financial panic will be "different" from all the previous ones. The difference, of course, is that the next hiccup is going to completely and totally wipe you out unless you have a stack of gold bars in your basement…which they or one of their (probably affiliated) sponsors will gladly sell to you!

Seriously, if you are really that concerned about an impending apocalypse, then you should rush out and buy seeds, water sources, and guns & ammo! Gold will be useless. You can't eat gold. And, it's not as if your new normal life in this post-apocalyptic wasteland will mean that you'll be carting around behind you a wagon full of gold bars to buy gas and groceries. If the magnitude of the mess people like Fröbe pitch became the norm, then there wouldn't be any gas to pump or bread to buy. And, that's the irony of the sales pitch of the "gold bugs". It's something right out of a George Romero movie plot.

The notion that the global financial system will come to a screeching halt for everybody on Earth except those few geniuses who had the foresight to trade out of stocks and into physical gold is ludicrous. But, this was the pitch that Fröbe made to Greg.

For most Americans, gold promotion comes in the form of television commercials featuring a "noted economic expert" or trusted television actor who shouts in a frantically aggressive manner and cautions the audience about impending doom and gloom. The audience is encouraged to visit a website for more information. When you get there, the first thing you see in big, bold type are the words, "US National Debt". Just below that is a digital "debt clock" displaying a number in the tens-of-trillions of dollars; representing the country's growing obligations. The numbers on the clock whirl past you manically, growing by tens of thousands of dollars per second. The intent is to unnerve you. Gold is sold by appealing to people's fears and the assault comes at you with unbridled enthusiasm.

In his phone conversation with Greg, Auric Fröbe said that after a financial market crash, Greg's stocks and bonds would be worthless. The breakdown of the international monetary system would also render his cash not worth the paper it was printed on. The only thing left that would have any value would be gold. For this reason, Greg needed to buy the precious metal as soon as possible! And, this was a scary thought for him.

The reason the pitch for gold has to be scary is that the case can't be made that it is a better long-term investment than a well-diversified portfolio of common stocks. Gold is a great investment only in the case of hyperinflation, a worldwide financial panic, or a zombie apocalypse. In other words, gold seems a great place to hide money if you are afraid that the status quo is about to end. The problem with this is that the only way you can profit from your investment is if you sell your gold down the road to someone who is even more afraid of the status quo than you were when you made the investment.

When you compare the return on investment between gold and the overall US stock market, there's not much of a contest. Stocks win hands down. Take a look at the chart below comparing the CAGR of gold and stocks. Going back nearly fifty years, you see that stocks have outperformed gold by a factor of three. To put that into dollars and cents, $10,000 invested in gold at the end of 1971 would have grown to more than $277,000 by the end of May 2017. That same investment in the stock market would have accumulated to $847,476.

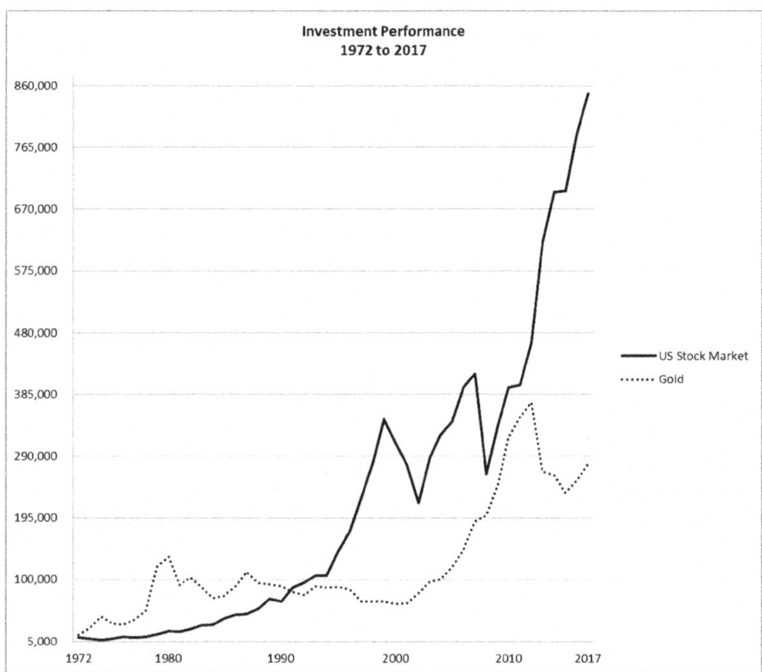

Sources: US Stock Market – CRSP Market Decile 1-10 1972-1992, Vanguard Total Stock Market Index Fund (VTSMX) 1993-2015. Gold – KITCO returns (kitco.com) 1972-2004, GLD ETF 2004-2015.

While the long-term historical outperformance of stocks relative to gold is pretty dramatic, the gold bugs would tell you that the chart above doesn't tell the whole story. They might say it's from fake statistics. They would also say that the real value of gold is how it outperforms the stock market when inflation is a problem.

Now, in reality, inflation hasn't been a problem since the early 1980s. But, you never know, inflation could become a problem in the future, just as a zombie apocalypse could. So, let's look at that (inflation, not the zombie apocalypse).

The chart below shows the percentage return of gold versus the US stock market since the end of 1971, not chronologically, but by the rate of inflation. On the left side of the chart is where inflation is highest. In 1979, it was at 13.29%. On the right side of the chart is where inflation is lowest. In 2008, it came in at just 0.09%. The chart does show that gold provided a higher investment return than stocks in a few years when inflation was high. But, that's not the whole story.

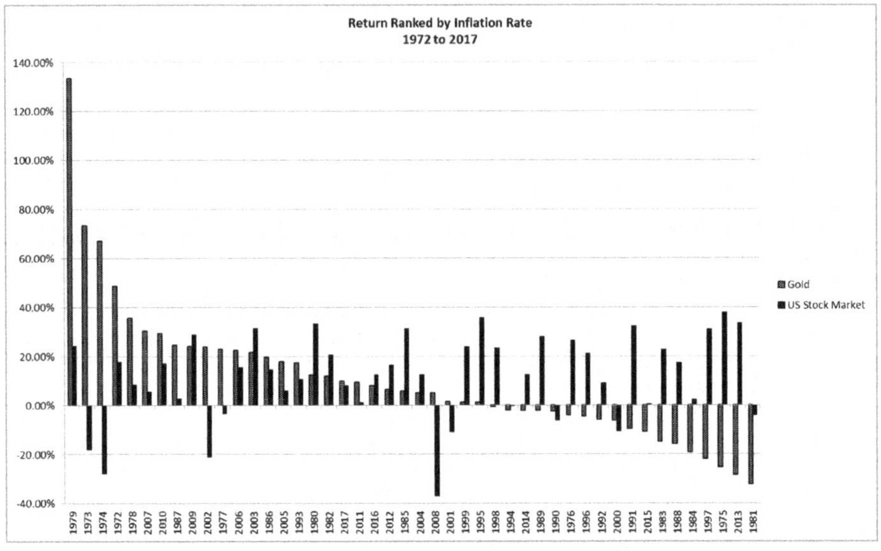

Sources: Ibid.

Inflation can't take all the credit for the huge return gold provided in 1979. For those of you who don't remember, that was the year of the Iran Hostage Crisis, the second Energy Crisis, and a time when the dollar was at an all-time low against the German Mark. The Irish Republican Army was blowing up hotels in Dublin and assassinating diplomats. China invaded Vietnam and the Soviet Union invaded Afghanistan. There was a lot of fear and anxiety – which is the kind of stuff that ends up in the sales pitch that guys like Auric Fröbe make for gold.

But, when you look back at the nearly fifty-year history represented in the chart above you see that stocks outperform gold more than half the time and provide investors with a higher average CAGR; beating the precious metal by 2.68%...and again, that number compounds over the entire timeframe depicted above.

It's also important to note that since the end of the 17th century, inflation in the United States has averaged just 3.22%. From the beginning of 1972 to the end of May 2017, it averaged about 4.00%. As such, one could argue that the longer-term trend for inflation is lower, not higher. So, unless there really is a zombie apocalypse, you're better off being invested in stocks than you are gold, even when the financial markets get a little scary.

So What Should You Do?

Look, I definitely understand the attraction of gold. I lived and worked in Saudi Arabia for a while and became mesmerized by the souk[7]. Part-street market, part-fashionable indoor shopping mall, these arcades are the pinnacle of tribute to the precious metal. The gold souk is lined with rows and rows of shops; some large others tiny. The shops line both sides of a long narrow alley and the bazaar has been in near constant operation since the 14th century.

The various boutiques offer everything from the most refined pieces of exquisite jewelry and purest gold nuggets to unprocessed rocks that have visible traces of silver, copper, or iron in them. In some shops, trinkets are placed in pretty felt-lined boxes. In others, the gold is sold by the ounce, actually the kilogram, without regard for craftsmanship or style; it's then placed in a brown paper sack as if the customer was buying a bagel and coffee on the way to work. The entryways of some kiosks are strung with curtains of gold chain that catch the sun and twinkle like the lights on a Christmas tree as you enter. In others the lustrous yellow metal is piled haphazardly into plastic trays like so many M&Ms poured into a candy dish.

I felt like a kid in a candy store each time I entered the souk. In the Middle East and Central Asia, gold is the measure of wealth, and women wear bangles of it from their wrists to their elbows. I certainly bought my share of the shiny stuff while I was there.

Gold has an allure like nothing else on Earth. It has for all of recorded history. And, it is certainly a valuable commodity. It's just not a great investment – especially when it is pitched as an alternative to a

7 An Arab market or marketplace; a bazaar.

well-diversified durable portfolio of financial assets. Gold does appear to offer a hedge against inflation, but the fact of the matter is that you probably already own other things that do too.

Some of these assets you may own outright, like your house, other real estate, or fine art. Others may be hidden away in your investment portfolio. Anyone who owns an S&P 500 index fund already has exposure to lots of inflation-hedging hard assets, including crude oil, precious metals, and real estate. For this reason, owning physical gold is unnecessary for most individual investors.

For clients that insist on having some exposure to physical gold, our advice is anchored in the Investment Philosophy I introduced in Chapter One. We would rely on historical data to inform the proper exposure of a wide class of commodities (beyond just precious metals, and specifically beyond just gold) to be included in a well-diversified portfolio of financial assets.

In its 2006 white paper, Strategic Asset Allocation and Commodities, Ibbotson Associates concluded that the Efficient Frontier (the point at which one can increase long-term investment returns without adding more risk) for a well-diversified portfolio of financial assets could be improved with the inclusion of a separate also well-diversified portfolio of commodities. And, depending on the mix of the financial assets in the base portfolio, the allocation to commodities ranged from 0% to 31%.

But, now I've got to stop and explain what all that means. The Ibbotson study said that you could theoretically improve your returns if you included a basket of various commodities in your portfolio's asset mix. Here's the rub.

The average improvement in return that the exposure to commodities provided was between 0.35% and 0.77%. That seems like little improvement for all the fuss. And, that's part of the reason we believe that most individual investors generally don't need to include commodities as an additional asset class in their investment portfolios. This is especially the case for clients with less than a million dollars in investable assets.

But, after all of that, if you still really want to own gold, then you should consider the various ways to do that. Gold, or any precious metal for that matter, can be purchased in a few ways. You can buy the physical bullion from any one of the zillions of Auric Fröbes out there. You can buy coins at lots of places; from local dealers to online wholesalers to garage sales and flea markets (if you know what you're doing). There are also "virtual" alternatives to owning the physical commodity.

There are gold-specific mutual funds and exchange-traded funds. Investors can also buy individual mining and minerals stocks. There are lots of them listed on the New York Stock Exchange and still more available on the NASDAQ over-the-counter market.

But, our advice would be to just not give in to such temptations and stick with the security and peace of mind that a well-diversified, passive investment portfolio will provide. Never lose sight of the fact that investments should not be made because you have a specific "feeling" about something. Investments should be made with the intent to finance your desired lifestyle in the future.

The Bottom Line

If an investment pitch or an ad for an investment needs to yell at you to get your attention, then it's probably a bad investment idea to listen to. Gold is sold by fear with unbridled enthusiasm, but it's not a great investment in and of itself.

If you like gold for its intrinsic qualities, then buy jewelry. If you're a collector, then buy rare coins. But, don't confuse these pieces of precious metal as investments, even if some day they are worth more money than you actually paid for them. Other than in these two ways, gold has no utility value.

In his 2014 book, The 5 Mistakes Every Investor Makes and How to Avoid Them: Getting Investing Right, Peter Mallouk said one important thing that we agree with:

"Gold belongs only in the portfolios of fear mongers and speculators. If you own gold in your portfolio, expect to not get paid an income, pay higher taxes on your returns, take a more volatile ride than the stock market, and get a long-term return lower than bonds."

CHAPTER 7

THE GOLDEN GIRL IN HER GOLDEN YEARS

The Drink's on Him

WE MET SOPHIA Petrillo only recently. She came to one of our live events and introduced herself after its conclusion. Apparently, she thought she'd be getting a free chicken dinner, which she didn't; more about that later.

Sophia is very sharp at 80 years of age, although she is a little quirky. She is also a master of the double entendre. It's impossible to tell if she intends to say the things she says or if the little devil does it intentionally just to see the reaction of the people around her. In either case, she can definitely get away with it and it is a marvelous thing to watch. She's a hoot. Sophia is also one of the healthiest octogenarians I know. She still skis and she spends a lot of time outdoors…I hope to be like that when I am 80! I'm sure she has many fun years ahead of her—a thoroughly delightful woman.

While we were standing there in the hotel meeting room Sophia told us that her (then) current advisor had suggested to her that she take half of her current liquid assets and invest them in an annuity. Before I go any further, this is probably a good place to explain these things.

An annuity is a contract between you and an insurance company. Your side of the contract is to put up some money, which the insurance company invests for you. The insurance company's contractual obligation is to pay a guaranteed income stream to you over a period of time. The sum total of those payments includes the return of your money plus whatever the insurance company's investments earn for you. The duration of those payments can be either fixed or flexible. They can come to you over a set number of years or over the course of your lifetime. Your annuity contract can either begin immediately or be deferred.

An immediate annuity starts paying out to you almost immediately after you hand over the investment money to the insurance company (see how clever investment terminology is!). A deferred annuity lets the investment money marinate over time before the income stream starts. Both immediate and deferred annuities can be either fixed or variable depending on the type of investments you tell the insurance company you want. I'll go into more detail on that later.

Sophia's broker suggested that she buy a deferred variable annuity. Now, remember, he told her that it would be a good idea to take half of all of her liquidity – the money she used to live on – and put it into that contract. Here's the odd thing about this. Sophia already had other annuities. The addition of this new one would have taken the amount of money she had in annuity assets to 75% of her total investment portfolio.

Yikes! This was wrong on so many levels.

First, accepted standards suggest that at most 50% of a person's investable assets should be allocated to annuities. Sophia had few remaining liquid assets. She already had a federal pension and was receiving social security. So, generating more guaranteed income at the risk of illiquidity was just plain unnecessary. If the broker had gone through the math with Sophia, or had tried to find out more about her specific situation, he wouldn't in good conscience have recommended such a course of action. Whatever the broker's ethics, according Sophia, he was a "Dunderhead".

"His advice to me was, 'you can protect your money and play the market at the same time,'" she said.

Sophia also told us that the dunderheaded broker was also off-putting. In her last meeting with him, she said that he had been wearing an old rumpled cardigan sweater and blue jeans. His shoes were scuffed penny loafers; the left one sans penny. He was drinking cranberry juice out of a mason jar and the lavender short-sleeve shirt and orange tie he was wearing both were stained by either his current tasty beverage or one he had consumed the last time he wore the ensemble.

"But, he was generous," Sophia said.

I wasn't sure if this was one of her double entendres, but I took the bait and asked what she meant.

"He poured some of the cranberry juice out of the mason jar into a paper cup and offered it to me. I accepted the cup, but didn't drink from it. None of this inspired confidence," she said.

The second reason the broker's recommendation was wrong for Sophia was because of what it would have cost her. Fees for annuity contracts vary. But, generally they are a more expensive option than other investment opportunities. Bear in mind that annuities are investment vehicles wrapped in a blanket of insurance. And, as I mentioned in Chapter One, each layer of an investment product has its own separate layer of fees and expenses. That's why the cost of variable annuities is higher than for fixed annuities.

All annuities have mortality fees and administrative expenses. These are essentially the cost of the insurance policy's death benefit. But, variable annuities also include the separate and various fees associated with the investments (typically a mutual fund) within the annuity. These internal fees can easily exceed 1.25% annually. And, it's not unusual to see fees of 3 or more percent per year. What makes the fees even more egregious is the fact that there is no – and I mean no – transparency regarding them.

I once spent hours trying to ferret out the various fees in a variable annuity contract that a new client owned. In an effort to fulfill my fiduciary duty, I wanted to understand what the client was paying and whether continuing to hold it was in his best interest. Some of the fees were buried deep in the fine print. Others were completely absent from the documents altogether; only vague references to things like commissions, underwriting fees, and actuarial fees. Nowhere in the contract was it mentioned that beneficiaries who inherit an annuity don't get a step up in basis.

Okay, the third reason the pitch to Sophia was wrong was that her investment choices were limited by the variable annuity company. What made matters worse was that an election had to be made regarding the allocation of the mutual funds within the annuity. Sadly, Dunderhead offered Sophia no help with this. As has been my experience with many clients who have brought in variable annuities at the outset of our relationship, Sophia had very little understanding of what the investment options were or how they could be allocated…let alone how they *should be* allocated.

Fourth, as with most variable annuities, the one Dunderhead tried to sell to Sophia included a Guaranteed Minimum Withdrawal Benefit, or GMWB. This separate rider (an add-on provision, which one has to pay for, of course) would have guaranteed Sophia that she could withdraw a specific percentage of the annuity's value every year until the value of the contract was exhausted. And, she would have had this right regardless of the annuity's investment performance. The contract offered a second rider providing her a Guaranteed Minimum Income Benefit. What the GMIB would have given her was a guaranteed level of income over her lifetime, again regardless of how the investments performed. These were non-cancellable riders and would have cost Sophia an extra one-half to three-quarters of a percent every year.

Now, in reality, the GMWB might pay off if Sophia invested in a highly risky – completely inappropriate – asset allocation. The allocation necessary for the GMWB to make sense would require an all-stock portfolio, which as a practical matter would require a fifteen to twenty-year holding period to achieve its (long-term) expected rate of return. For Sophia, this wasn't practical. Remember that she's 80!

For an investor in his or her 40s or even mid-sixties, holding an investment for that duration is quite reasonable. It's important to remember that although annuities don't include an upfront sales change, they all have deferred surrender charges. In other words, they charge a percentage of your investment for a period of between 5 to 10 years if you want to withdraw your money. So, should you decide to purchase an annuity, you need to be in it for the long haul. The fact of the matter is that for such an investor, it renders the added cost of the two riders a complete and total waste of money. The reason for this is that the US stock market has provided investors with a CAGR of right around 10% since 1926. That's more than enough return to be able to grow the assets to a level where there will be more than sufficient funds available to make future withdrawals over and above any minimums the riders would have guaranteed.

There's No Free Lunch

I have met with far too many retirees with too few liquid assets because everything they had saved was in an annuity…or two…or even more. These clients were obviously sold investments without consideration of their existing portfolios and likely without any real knowledge of their future retirement needs. I can envision most of these contracts being written up between the entree and dessert rounds at an "educational seminar".

How many of you have received those invitations in the mail that include a fabulous "gourmet meal" at a local chain restaurant? Seriously, can a chain restaurant really serve a gourmet meal? These invitations typically come from a local "financial expert" who offers you a free chicken dinner and an opportunity to hear about the benefits of owning annuities. The invitation says that you'll learn how you can get tax-deferred "risk-free" capital appreciation, "guaranteed" income, and life insurance all for one low cost!

When you get there, the financial expert turns out to be an insurance salesman who talks for about an hour or so before the meal. He'll often be a very personable, likable, funny, and sincere chap. He will exude confidence, poise, knowledge, and credibility. He will ooze sincerity. His shiny white teeth may even reflect light back at you like the good guy in an old western movie. He will come across as honorable, ethical, and trustworthy.

Okay, maybe he'll be all of those things, or maybe not. Just remember that when you get there, that free meal is going to come at a cost. Hey, it's not like this guy works for the Albert Schweitzer Financial Services Company. You are there to be sold. The cost of the rubber chicken dinner is just a cost of doing business. And, the business is selling annuities!

In fairness, some are better than others (the insurance salesman, not the chicken dinner). But, I still don't understand how an advisor can get up in front of a bunch of complete and total strangers and pitch them on a product when he can't have the foggiest notion of what's in their best interest. Trust me; the odds are exceptionally high that at least a few of the people in the audience will buy something from this guy at the end of the "seminar". And, this guy will gladly take the order (and the commission)! And, he'll do this whether an investment in an annuity is appropriate for them or not.

"I Would Die & Go to Hell Before I Would Sell an Annuity"

A prominent investment advisor has made hating annuities one of his primary marketing strategies. And, quite frankly his television commercials are bizarrely entertaining. His pitch, and that's exactly what it is, is quite simple. His firm doesn't sell annuities – and they never will. Well, duh!

That's because his firm is not in that business. So, the commercials, while fun to watch, are just slightly misleading. You can't make an apples-to-apples comparison between what his firm does and what an annuity does. They're just not the same thing. He may as well say that he would die and go to hell before selling kittens. After all, his firm isn't in the kitten business. But, that doesn't make kittens bad.

I single this guy out only because his commercials are funny; weird, but funny. And, the reality is that there is an almost cult-like following among financial advisors…of every ilk…who loathe annuities. There is even an entire organization among fee-only financial advisors that eschews any type of commission-based investment product…including (maybe especially) annuities. The association actually mandates that its members sign and annually renew a "Fiduciary Oath" promising that they won't even show to a client any financial product that charges a fee or commission.

I don't know if this stems from profound guilt, a self-impressed feeling of piety, purity, and superiority, or a simple lack of knowledge. Maybe the group is just made up of like-minded folks who merely don't have an interest in using annuities to help clients plan for retirement. They gather together with this common interest in the same way smokers congregate outside office buildings enjoying their cigarettes without an interest or concern about how it affects the people entering and leaving the building. Whatever the reason, I am simply surprised by the intensity of the hatred.

As an owner of a fee-only registered investment advisory firm, my role is to be a fiduciary. ***Not only does that mean that I have to put my clients' interests above my own, I take it to mean that I have to put their interests above my biases!*** I mentioned in Chapter Five that our firm neither loves nor hates any particular financial product. We neither encourage nor discourage anything. We recommend strategies and the products that help achieve them when they make sense and discourage them when they don't.

Just because our firm is a fee-only registered investment adviser doesn't mean that we should be expected to go along with what I feel is misplaced industry groupthink that holds annuities in such disdain. The idea that an advisor would refuse to include annuities as a tool to help clients plan for retirement is analogous to the proverbial "fighting with one hand tied behind your back".

It is the responsibility of the advisor to use annuities judiciously. Annuities can benefit clients but only when used in moderation in the context of a holistic financial plan for life. Clients benefit when we act in their best interests. The real issue with annuities is simply that they are often sold, and the operative word here is ***sold***, incorrectly and inappropriately.

So What Should You Do?

Annuities are complicated. That's why they can be confusing to the average investor (and lots of financial advisors too). They clearly are not for everyone, but when used properly can be an effective tool to augment retirement income.

As I mentioned above, an annuity is an insurance contract. Like other forms of insurance, an annuity offers a death benefit to your heirs when you pass away. But, unlike other forms of insurance, an annuity's main purpose isn't to provide indemnity protection. It is to create an income stream. That's it; plain and simple. The mechanism for this is likewise plain and simple.

When you buy an annuity, you're giving money to the insurance company to make investments for your benefit. In exchange, the insurance company guarantees you an income stream that will pay out to you over a set number of years or for the remainder of your life. There are even versions that will pay out over the course of both your life and your spouse's life.

The differences between the various types of annuities, their features, and their benefits aren't really germane to this book. But, what is relevant is how they can be used in the context of cash flow management in retirement.

Because annuities are considered a type of retirement plan, the income and capital appreciation they enjoy are not taxable to you during the accumulation phase of the contract. This is the period of time before you start taking money out. So, your money grows tax-deferred. When you begin to take distributions out of an annuity (the annuitization phase) that money will be partially taxable. The degree to which distributions are taxed is based on the relative proportion in each payment between the return of your own capital and the underlying investments' appreciation. Before you start taking money out, the growth doesn't get taxed.

This is one of the key benefits of annuities. Used in conjunction with other, traditional retirement savings plans like an IRA, a 401 (k), or an employer sponsored pension, an annuity can be used to augment retirement income.

For our clients still planning for retirement our advice is that they ***always*** maximize their deductible contributions to qualified retirement plans before entertaining the notion of buying an annuity. But, for those clients with the means, who have "maxed out" those available plans, an annuity may be appropriate.

For those still working and saving for retirement, the fact that an annuity will grow on a tax-deferred basis is of major benefit to many clients. And, our advice to them is to leave those annuity assets alone undisturbed for fifteen to twenty years so that (as I noted above) they can achieve their expected rate of return.

The point here is that if the use of an annuity will help optimize the client's planning picture, then we'll use one (or more) in the implementation of that plan. In those circumstances where an annuity can't be used optimally, they are not considered. Furthermore, in the cases where an annuity makes good financial planning sense, we test to make sure that the client's liquidity won't be negatively impacted over that fifteen to twenty-year accumulation period as a result of owning that contract. The last thing we want to see happen is for a client to tap into the annuity to cover living expenses at any point during that time.

Annuities provide a reliability factor that no bond or equity market exposure can produce consistently. I don't know of any investment other than an annuity that can provide a fixed amount of income over an individual's lifetime – let alone do it on a guaranteed[8] basis. For

8 It is important to note that the "guarantee" is made by the insurance company.

many working Americans, the gradual disappearance of corporate pensions will continue to create a gap in reliable retirement income. Annuities can be used to fill this gap. That's what makes them a valuable tool in planning for the distribution phase (retirement) of one's personal investment cycle.

Before investing retirement assets in an annuity, you need to do your homework (or you can hire our firm and we'll do the legwork for you). Research cost and buy judiciously. In general, it makes sense to avoid variable annuities. The annual fees alone can make them a bad investment. Look for a fixed index annuity or if interest rates continue to rise consider a deferred fixed annuity. Above all, understand their purpose in your investment portfolio. They are not a good fit for everyone and much depends on your personal situation, risk tolerance, and other sources of income.

Not all annuities are expensive, but variable annuities are typically more so than the fixed version. In general, your goal should be to own a contract that has annual fees and expenses at or below 2% per year. Many annuities, especially single premium immediate annuities, deferred-income annuities, and fixed-rate annuities have very low fees and many have low or no annual fees. Index annuities have annual fees that are on par with other types of fee-based managed portfolios. As such, the assumption that annuities are bad because they all come with high fees is an overgeneralization. An annuity should be assessed on its value based on the cost of other types of investments.

For those who have a difficult time restraining their spending in retirement, an annuity could act as a tool that restricts the outflow of assets. Most annuities allow for a withdrawal of only 10% per year without penalties. And, once annuitized (when the guaranteed income benefit is activated) the funds distributed are locked in and can't be changed.

The Bottom Line

Annuities do have their place in a long-term financial plan when owned as a vehicle to augment retirement income. When viewed in the context of "a personal" pension, a fixed or deferred annuity can make sense in the right circumstances.

As you plan for retirement, never lose sight of what former boxer George Foreman said about it. *"The question isn't at what age I want to retire, it's at what income."*

CHAPTER 8

THE JUNK BOND KING AND I

A Trip Down Memory Lane

ANNA LEONOWENS WAS a tall, stout woman. Prim, proper, maybe a bit stuffy, I could envision her being cast as the schoolmarm in a period film on 19th-century British colonialism. She spoke proper English flawlessly in the accent of the Queen herself. Anna didn't seem to have a sense of humor and exuded a sense of rugged individualism and determination. While her situation wasn't bleak, it wasn't optimal either. Nevertheless, I felt that she would persevere.

Anna came to see me early in my career hoping that I could help her out of a bad situation. In retrospect, it was one of the saddest encounters I have had in this business. Anna's husband, Thomas, had recently passed away and the widow sought my advice because she wasn't sure what to make of the investment portfolio he had put together.

The portfolio, constructed at the advice of Thomas's broker, consisted of a number of long-term individual corporate bonds. The face value of the whole portfolio (the amount that would be redeemed when the individual bonds ultimately matured) was $200,000. In the early

1980s that was a great deal of money. It would have been the equivalent of nearly $600,000 today. The problem that Anna had was this: The brokerage statements she was receiving showed that the market value of the bonds was considerably lower than their face value. The bonds weren't worth anything near what Thomas had paid for them.

Thomas made the investments sometime in the early 1970s thinking that bonds were the best and safest investment he could get. His broker clearly agreed, and likely encouraged the purchases, feeding into Thomas's own perceptions about fixed income securities. I really don't know for sure. After all, I wasn't there. But, I can envision what the broker's message may have been.

"Thomas, my boy, bonds are safe. They're guaranteed. All you have to do is buy high-quality paper issued by solid, blue-chip companies and you can't lose. It doesn't matter what happens to interest rates between now and then, because you get all your money back when the bonds mature. You're not buying a stock that has risk. With bonds, you're just loaning money to the company, which will pay you back everything you lent to it when the bonds mature. In the meantime, they're also going to pay you a nice fat two-percent on the loan."

To a certain extent, the broker's message was accurate, but only to a point. I'll get to that later. For now, I want to explain why the bonds in that portfolio lost value.

There are three components that determine the value of a bond. The first component is the stated interest rate on the instrument. The second is the time left until the bond matures. And, the third is the market rate of interest right now.

Let's say that you buy a bond today and its stated rate of interest is 3%. The bond matures in 30 years. This is a newly-issued bond and is priced at the market rate of interest, which is 3%. So, if the face value of the bond is $1,000, then you'll pay $1,000 for it. The interest you will receive is $30 per year.

If interest rates on thirty-year bonds go down to (let's say) 2%, then your bond is going to be worth more money than $1,000. The reason for this is that the market rate of interest (the rate borrowers would pay to investors) is lower than what your bond would pay to those same investors if you sold it to them. So, you can demand more than $1,000 because your bond pays more than the market rate of interest. Investors that buy bonds from new issuers would receive $20 a year in interest payments. An investor that bought the bond from you would receive $30 a year. Your bond would pay the new owner $10 per year more for the 30-year life of the bond. That's why bonds generally increase in value when interest rates decline. The exact same thing happens in reverse when interest rates rise.

When Thomas originally bought the bonds interest rates were between 2% and 3%. By today's standards those rates of return may not seem too bad. But, between the time the investments were made and the day that Anna came in to see me, interest rates had risen dramatically. From late 1976 to mid-1980 the Federal Funds rate had risen from 4.17% to 10.39%. Interest rates on 30-year bonds were even higher.

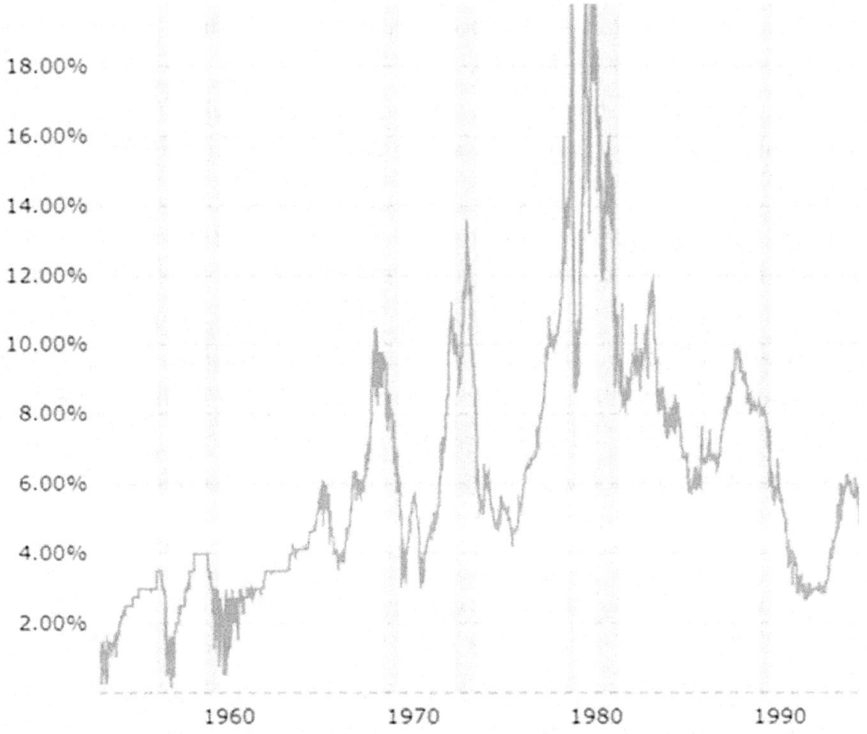

Source: Macrotrends, LLC

What made matters worse for Anna was that the portfolio generated interest income of less than $6,000 a year at a time when inflation was running at nearly 15%. She didn't have enough to live on and the cost of goods was soaring. The frustrating part for me was the fact that I could do nothing to help her.

If Anna sold all the bonds, she would have taken a loss of nearly $90,000. What would have been left over could have generated a little more income for her, given that interest rates had risen so much. But, the incremental interest income would never compensate her for the loss of principal, which would be impossible to recoup. She ended up going back to work as a nanny.

Turning Junk into Treasure...Not!

Tuptim Moreno is a smart, well-read 86-year-old self-made woman. Born into a family of modest means, the feisty Tuptim is a widow, just like Anna. I think that Anna and Tuptim probably have more in common than just that, but I've never asked.

Tuptim moves from place to place a bit delicately, but she is very sure-footed. My sense is that she was a dancer in another life. Her sleek, still-toned body clearly suggests this. She carries a cane with her, but never uses it for support. It's more of prop used to show people that she can fend for herself unaided by anyone or anything. She's also a quiet, deep-thinking lady. In answer to most of my questions Tuptim typically begins her reply by pursing her full lips and murmuring, "hmm".

When Tuptim came in to meet me she brought with her the documents I had requested when we spoke over the phone. Chief among this paperwork was a recent copy of her brokerage statement.

"Tell me, Tuptim, what led you to make these investments," I asked in that first meeting.

"I simply followed the advice of my broker. Why?"

I told her that I was curious about how the broker determined the portfolio's asset allocation and how he arrived at the specific investments in the account.

"Hmm, I don't recall. I do remember that he said that the funds would be very well diversified. The initial conversation was pretty quick and he seemed to know what I needed more than I did."

Really?

So, this clairvoyant clown knew better what Tuptim needed than she did? And, he came to this revelation without asking her anything about her personal situation or other resources? This begs the question: just how well did this advisor know this client?

The answer is obviously, not very well. Tuptim's portfolio actually wasn't diversified at all. There was a lot of stock market exposure in the account even though the asset allocation was divided roughly 50/50 between stocks and bonds. Broker Bozo put Tuptim into various actively-traded mutual funds. A little more than half of them were invested in large-cap domestic stocks. The remainder was invested in a bevy of high-yield bond funds; perhaps to beef up Tuptim's income. But, whatever the reason, the bonds were not there to serve their intended purpose. I'll explain that later. The more troubling issue was that there was nothing in Tuptim's account to protect her from stock market volatility. The reason for this is that high-yield bonds behave more like stocks than bonds.

High-yield bonds, otherwise appropriately referred to as "junk bonds" are corporate debt obligations that are rated below investment grade. The reason they behave like stocks is that their value is more directly tied to the fortunes of the issuing company than to changes in interest rates. Junk bonds are not issued by big, solid, blue-chip corporations. They are issued by smaller, weaker, riskier enterprises. So, as a practical matter, the 50/50 split between stocks and bonds in Tuptim's account exposed her to the risk of an all-equity portfolio – half of which was invested in companies whose creditworthiness was less than investment grade.

So What Should You Do?

Okay, so let's get to the heart of the matter. Bonds serve just two purposes in an investment portfolio. The first is to provide safe, reliable income. The second is to provide ballast.

The income purpose is straightforward. There is a stated rate of interest on every bond and, in general, investors can expect that interest to be paid to them semi-annually until the bond matures. When the bond does mature, the investor will receive its face value. If the face value of the bond is $1,000, then that's what the issuing company will pay back at maturity. The likelihood that an investor will receive semi-annual interest payments and get his or her money back at maturity increases with the creditworthiness of the issuing company. The higher the credit rating is, the greater the certainty of payment. Bankrupt companies don't pay interest!

The ballast purpose is also pretty straightforward. Stocks and bonds provide investors with different (expected) rates of return and different levels of (expected) risk. Over very long periods of time, the investment returns from stocks have been higher than those from bonds. This higher level of investment performance has come at the cost of a higher level of risk. One way to lower the overall risk in an all-stock investment portfolio is to include some bonds. In general, the higher the proportion of bonds added to the portfolio, the lower the risk of loss over time. In other words, the key determinant of a given portfolio's expected risk and return all boils down to the asset-allocation decision.

That's why bonds play such an important role in portfolio construction. They smooth out some of the volatility and add to a portfolio's diversification. But, they are not without risk! Most advisors know this but do a very poor job of communicating it to clients. There are three main risks to owning a bond: credit risk; interest rate risk; and, purchasing power risk.

Credit risk is the easiest to understand. This is the risk that a company might default on its debt. The higher the rating is, the lower the likelihood of default. A company with a high credit rating will have a solid balance sheet and history of making good on its obligations. Think of a company's credit rating like your FICO credit score.

Earlier I discussed a component of interest rate risk. This was the hazard that plagued Anna. But, there's more to it than just a change in rates. The remaining time left until a bond's maturity exacerbates interest rate risk. The longer the time until redemption, the greater the effect a change in interest rates will have on a bond.

When Anna came in to visit me, the average life remaining on her portfolio was still close to twenty years. Thomas had purchased bonds with very long maturities. His broker may have recommended this in an effort to increase the portfolio's income. Long-term bonds pay more than short-term bonds. But, they also have more interest rate risk. Because the broker failed to explain that, Thomas unwittingly purchased a ticking time bomb and never knew it. By the time Anna and I met, the bomb had already exploded.

The third risk in a bond comes about over time as inflation eats into the value of the dollar. Inflation erodes purchasing power and the fixed rate of interest on a bond rarely compensates an investor for this. By the time a bond matures, the investor is paid in dollars that buy fewer goods than they did when the investment was made. This risk is more severe for long-term bonds than it is for short-term bonds. This was the other reason Anna was forced back to work.

For most investors, rising interest rates and high inflation are little more than subjects from a history book. It's easy to forget that bonds have interest rate risk because they have been in a 30-year bull market. We haven't had high inflation for so long that it has been easy to forget its effect on fixed income securities.

In recent years, however, interest rates have been slowly creeping higher. At some point in the future, their advance may increase in size and speed. While this is no reason to avoid bonds in well-diversified durable portfolios, investors need to be judicious about what they buy.

Our advice when buying individual bonds is to ladder portfolios of individual bonds with consistent annual maturities beginning with one year and extending out (in some appropriate cases) all the way to 20- or 30-years. In other words, structure the ladder so that some bonds mature every single year beginning next year.

The bulk of the ladder should be made up of intermediate term bonds so that the average life of the portfolio is between seven and ten years. In this way, the average life can be shortened or extended as warranted by changes in interest rates over time. This shortening or lengthening of average life is achieved as bonds mature and reinvesting their proceeds into either (well) shorter or longer bonds.

Purchasing bond mutual funds in another way to hold a diversified portfolio of bonds at varying lengths of maturity and interest. When investing in bond funds, check the internal expense ratio looking for those under .20%. I have seen bond funds with expenses over 1% which, of course, decreases the yield.

Using US Treasury securities instead of corporate bonds lowers the credit risk but often has lower yields. The difference in yield often does not compensate investors for the credit risk. In cases where Triple-A rated corporate bonds offer a yield advantage over Treasuries of the same maturity, they would be better than government bonds. In every case, I would stress quality and avoid non-investment-grade (junk) issuers.

My dislike of junk bonds is the result of two experiences. The first is that I have seen too many individuals harmed by brokers who advised them to use only high-yield bonds in the fixed-income allocation of their portfolios. As I noted in my discussion of Rita's situation, junk bonds do not serve the intended purposes that fixed-income securities have in a well-diversified durable portfolio. The second is of a more personal nature.

I began my investment career in the 1980s as a broker at Drexel Burnham Lambert, home of the "Junk Bond King," Michael Milken. What a wild ride that was!

Milken's office was in Beverly Hills, California where working on Wall Street means being in the office awfully early. The New York Stock Exchange opens for business in Lower Manhattan at 9:30 in the morning. That meant that Milken had to be on the phone by 6:30 a.m., Pacific Time. But, nobody moseyed in at that later hour.

The day in Beverly Hills began at 4:00 in the morning and everyone from traders to assistants to clerks were expected to be there prior to that. Tardiness was not tolerated and the demands on the staff were onerous. With the exception of Milken, his brother Lowell, and three other guys (Gary Winnick, Larry Fink, and Warren Trepp), everybody else had to ask permission to go to the bathroom.

The trading room of Drexel's Beverly Hills office was a stressful, chaotic echo chamber. The energy was exhilarating and terrifying. In the middle of the vast bullpen was a big "X-shaped" trading desk and at its center sat the Junk Bond King himself; telephone glued to one ear, another held in his free hand. Standing next to him was a young assistant holding several more phones, which he passed to Milken in a round robin as the trader finished each call. Between comments spoken softly into the phone Milken would bark orders at other traders, who in turn would bark other orders at still other traders, yelling back and forth between them, their assistants, and the clerks running around the "X" climbing over each other like swarming ants.

Nobody ever left the trading room floor; they were either forbidden or stayed for fear of losing their livelihood. The space was constantly attended by an in-house caterer who kept a smorgasbord of truly gourmet food available through the trading day. Perhaps this was intended to be a perk. As a practical matter, it really only ensured that nobody ever left the room.

The subterranean garage was every bit the spectacle. Next to the private elevator that led directly to the trading room floor were the reserved parking spaces of the King and his Court. Parked in the stalls were the sleekest sports cars from Italy and the most expensive luxury sedans from Germany and Great Britain, all owned by guys in their late twenties to mid-thirties. The avarice and arrogance were palpable and the lords of the "X-desk" were resplendent in them.

This was the "new normal" at the firm I had joined years earlier, and once loved. It was fueled by the ever-rising demand for high and higher yields and has left a negative feeling in me that I have not yet forgotten. I will admit that it has tainted my opinion of these investments. Despite my gut reaction to them, under the right circumstances, high-yield bonds can serve a purpose in a portfolio. But, they are inappropriate for a retired woman like Tuptim Moreno.

Because of their credit worthiness (or lack thereof) they can't be relied upon for safe, reliable cash flow (the way an investment grade bond can). Their risk/reward characteristics more closely resemble those of a common stock than they do a bond, so they fail on providing ballast. And, when an advisor suggests them to serve these roles, he or she is doing the client a great disservice! Junk bonds miss on both of the intended purposes of the asset class. These are the two main reasons that I don't like them.

Worse still for Tuptim was the fact that the equity component of her portfolio included high-fee mutual funds of mostly large-cap US stocks. Missing were any of the components of the Four-Factor Model we use to help clients diversify their accounts (as I introduced in Chapter One).

The Bottom Line

Our perspective is that security selection ought to be limited to passive investment vehicles tied to various benchmarks for the purpose of tracking the returns of those benchmarks as closely as possible, and to do it in a way that mitigates fees.

The main driver of long-term investment returns is the asset allocation of the portfolio. This is far more important than individual security selection. But, that's the part of the recipe that most financial advisors don't get. It is also the reason that many advisors recommend products to clients that are ultimately harmful to them.

Bonds have a place in a durable strategic asset allocation and the main objective of their inclusion should be risk mitigation. For investors in retirement, the right allocation of high-quality bonds of varying maturities in a portfolio is important. But as we learned from Anna, having all your eggs in a bond basket is not advisable.

Our position on using only high-quality bonds doesn't agree with the opinion once offered by the junk bond king when he said, *"The past is always Triple-A. We can all remember what the past was. But, if we try to make the future Triple-A, we have no future. The future is always Single-B."*

CHAPTER 9

WHAT A NICE COUPLE (OF TAX MYTHS & MISTAKES)

From Rags to Riches

Arnie and Lillian began their retirement planning right after his big promotion, when he landed an executive position and a huge salary increase, at the industrial fittings company where he had long been employed as a union laborer. Lillian was a stay-at-home mom. In addition to Arnie's 401 (k) plan he participated in his employer's pension, which gave him the opportunity to own shares of the company's stock.

The couple is careful and conservative, but when it came to saving for retirement, they were not overly cautious. Arnie's 401 (k) was invested in stock market index funds. As a result, the portfolio didn't generate any income. Dividend and capital gain distributions were automatically reinvested into the respective funds. As the couple neared retirement, they realized that changing their asset allocation was essential to generating income to replace Arnie's lost salary.

They interviewed various brokers and financial advisors before deciding to hire us. They asked each candidate what they would recommend to generate retirement income and if they could discuss the tax implications of taking lump-sum (one-time) distributions from Arnie's retirement plans. They also asked how the advisors' planning advice would evolve over the next five years as they intended to apply for Social Security benefits at age 70.

Now, I get the fact that it is not the role of a stockbroker or the twenty-something financial advisor who works at the local bank branch to offer tax advice or prepare a tax return. I also accept that these people aren't actuaries or Social Security experts. But, they have to have at least a semblance of understanding that the investment advice they offer is going to result in a transaction where money moves from one place to another, *potentially* (if not *actually*) resulting in a taxable event. They've got to know that at some point their clients are going to receive Social Security benefits and that those benefits are going to have an impact on the client's overall financial situation.

The amazing thing – as Arnie and Lillian found out – is that most financial advisors have no clue that (let alone how) their investment advice can impact someone's tax situation! Some of the kooky things Arnie and Lillian heard from the "professionals" they talked to included these priceless gems:

"Why worry about taxes? If you owe taxes it means you made money."

"Your tax burden will decrease in retirement."

"The stock in that pension plan should never be rolled into an IRA."

"The stock in that pension plan must be rolled into an IRA."

"Distributions from your IRA won't affect your taxes."

"Social Security benefits are not taxable."

"You should wait to get Social Security."

"You shouldn't wait to get Social Security."

"A Roth IRA has the exact same tax benefits as a regular IRA."

"The Required Minimum Distribution from your IRA can't be delayed."

"The Required Minimum Distribution has no special tax considerations."

Really?

I'll discuss each of these issues later in the chapter. For now, it's important to note that we feel pretty strongly that individual investors are best served by advisors that provide holistic financial guidance that takes the entirety of their financial situation into account. This clearly means understanding the tax ramifications of investment decisions. And, the only way this is possible is to truly understand the various rules and regulations governing investment gains and losses, qualified and non-qualified retirement plans, and Social Security. Only then can the advisor model various "what-if" scenarios that estimate a client's tax burden into the future. And, oh by the way, that's exactly what our firm does.

Girls Just Want to Have Fun

Carol and Susan are some of my favorite clients. They are full of life, outgoing, and smart. Carol is a retired 6th-grade teacher. Susan was a stay-at-home mom to their son Ben. Susan enjoys a comfortable pension from teaching and both women receive Social Security benefits. They have a more-than-modest, but not huge, investment portfolio. What makes Carol and Susan so interesting is that they are the most active, adventuresome sixty-somethings I know. The couple are definitely not afraid to take risks, which is part of why they became clients of ours.

The couple had an account at a major brokerage firm, a small portion of which was dedicated as their "speculative play money". The remainder was invested in actively-managed equity mutual funds.

The issue the couple had was that the trading account actually threw off a lot of short-term capital gains. Don't get me wrong, the broker racked up plenty of offsetting losses. But, there were a lot of gains. This presented them with some interesting planning issues that I'll go into more detail about later. Before I do, I want to introduce you to one other couple.

The Absent-Minded Professor

Ned Brainerd is a retired college professor. He and his wife Betsy never had kids, which may be why they are so happy and have so much money…just kidding. Their wealth is more the result of Ned's many wise real estate investments and his "notorious frugality". He earned the "Absent-Minded Professor" moniker because he gets so caught up in work that he often forgets very important things, like his wedding day (seriously, that actually happened). These days Ned is so caught up in his golf game that he still forgets lots of important matters.

Now, to be fair, many retired folks forget things. Sometimes this includes deadlines and dates that can have an impact on their financial situations. For example, April 15th is kind-of an important date, and most people understand and remember its significance. Others don't.

But, when it comes to financial matters, it is really important that one's financial advisor be attuned to what's going on in their clients' lives and be abreast of the deadlines and dates that, if missed, could have detrimental financial consequences. And, it just so happens that something like this happened to Ned and Betsy.

Ned is 80 years old now. Back when he was in his early seventies he began taking annual Required Minimum Distributions out of his IRA. This mandatory withdrawal has to be calculated and transferred to a taxable account before the end of every calendar year. And, you'd think that the financial advisor to a seventy-something-year-old guy would not just know that, but would be so attuned to it that he'd remind his absent-minded client over and over again. Well, in Ned's case, that didn't happen. Sadly, that mistake was costly for him. On the positive side, that's what prompted the couple to become clients of ours.

At our firm, we help clients prepare the schedule that calculates, what the IRS affectionately calls, the Required Minimum Distribution (RMD). We run the numbers for them every year. And, we make sure to take the distribution well in advance of the end of the year.

Now it's time to explain why all of this stuff matters and how it affected these three couples.

So What Should You Do?

In the case of Arnie and Lillian, there was no dumb advice given to the couple because they had not yet selected a financial advisor. But, during the course of their vetting process, they asked a lot of really great questions and ended up getting a lot of really bad answers. Had the couple selected an ill-informed or completely uninformed advisor, it could have had disastrous consequences. To get a better feel for that, let's take a closer look at some of the issues presented by answers they got.

Why Worry About Taxes?

The notion that you don't have to worry about taxes is the polar opposite of an equally stupid concept to which we've heard many other financial advisors espouse. Namely, that taxes are the only thing that you should be worried about. Both ideas are hogwash.

Taxes are the tail. Your whole financial well-being is the dog. Focusing solely on taxes is letting the tail wag the dog. That's just a dumb idea. It's accurate to say that people owe taxes because they make money, but it's also naive.

An individual's complex set of hopes, goals, wants, and dreams presents a kaleidoscope of interconnected tradeoffs. Financing those tradeoffs likewise presents an array of options that is every bit as complex. A financial advisor focused solely on "making money" will ultimately guide his or her client down a path that ignores too many variables that might be considered to help that individual optimize his or her entire financial gestalt.

To avoid this misstep, our firm works to connect the dots between consumption goals and financing opportunities (presented by each of the assets the client has) to make sure that the solutions we recommend are tempered to avoid giving one component more weight than it would otherwise deserve as we seek the optimal solution for that specific person.

Part of this work is to deliberately plan for a targeted tax rate in retirement. We can do this effectively only when a wealth-management oversight program is in place that takes into consideration pieces of the puzzle that may not otherwise seem to fit together. This includes things as mundane as making sure quarterly estimated tax payments are made, to having taxes withheld from Social Security benefits, pensions payouts, or retirement account withdrawals.

Your Tax Burden Will Decrease in Retirement

This comment by one of the advisors that Arnie and Lillian interviewed is absolutely correct...for some people. For a vast majority of others, however, this assumption is completely erroneous. And, that can be said of nearly every blanket statement that was made to the couple.

The fact is that there was no way in the world that financial advisor could possibly have known how Arnie and Lillian's tax situation was going to change. We didn't know until after weeks of analysis and several planning meetings. For many individual investors, taxes don't decline in retirement.

Many of the tax-mitigating opportunities that exist when one is working simply disappear at retirement. For most seniors, their biggest "tax break" – their home mortgage interest deduction – is gone by the time they retire. They will no longer be reducing income by contributing to a company 401 (k) and their opportunity to contribute to a deductible IRA ends at age 70 or when there is no longer income from work. Without the home mortgage interest deduction, most retirees find it difficult to accumulate enough other itemized deductions to get them over the threshold of the standard deduction. Things like business write-offs, mileage expenses, and dues and subscriptions all vanish.

Okay, so much for the generalizations made by many stockbrokers and other financial advisors. Let's look at the "advice" that was suggested to Arnie and Lillian regarding their specific tax situation.

Net Unrealized Appreciation (NUA)

This relates to the shares in Arnie's pension. There are specific tax rules that apply to company stock held in an employer-sponsored retirement plan and there were two advisors that weighed in on this topic. They both made blanket statements to Arnie and Lillian. One said that the shares should "never" be rolled into an IRA; the other said that they "must" be. Both are incorrect.

The reason for this is that those shares of stock could have been rolled into an IRA (this is the more common approach) or they could have been distributed out to a taxable account (this has special planning considerations). Nevertheless, either type of distribution is completely acceptable. But, the two bubbleheads that Arnie and Lillian talked to didn't understand the rule or its planning implications!

During our planning work, it became evident that the latter action was the most appropriate option for Arnie and Lillian. So, Arnie put the shares into a taxable account and the value of the distribution was taxed as ordinary income. But, it received favorable tax treatment. The stock wasn't valued using its market price on the date of the distribution. Instead, it was taxed using the plan's original cost basis.

Plan Basis	Arnie's Tax	Market Value
200,000	56,000	800,000

For Arnie & Lillian this was appealing given that they now had access to a very low-cost basis (i.e., highly appreciated) asset that they could use for income or to make charitable contributions. What's more, the couple would be relieved of the ongoing addition to post-retirement (taxable) income that would have resulted from having an additional $800,000 in an IRA. And, this gets me to the next crazy thing that Arnie & Lillian heard from one of the advisors they interviewed.

Distributions from Your IRA Won't Affect Your Taxes

Hooey! Of course they will. That makes this statement the second-dumbest thing that Arnie & Lillian heard from the candidates they interviewed. When you take money out of your IRA, it gets taxed at your marginal rate. The same applies to a pension or profit-sharing plan and a 401 (k). When money leaves a tax-deferred retirement account and goes into a taxable account, the distribution is taxable. This next one, though, is the hands-down dumbest comment they heard.

Social Security Benefits Are Not Taxable

Ah, yeah, they are! Although Social Security benefits for many Americans are not taxable, for others they are. The determining factor is the total level of income the person earns in a given year. In the case of Arnie and Lillian, fully 85% of their benefits are taxable. This is often the case for people taking distributions from IRAs with substantial balances. And, this is a situation that we encounter (and solve) frequently in our practice.

Between 0 to 85 percent of Social Security benefits are taxable if certain income levels are met. Currently, those filing a joint return are taxed on Social Security at varying levels if their Adjusted Gross Income (AGI) is over $32,000. For a single taxpayer, that threshold is $25,000. Benefits became taxable with the last major overhaul of Social Security benefits. These income levels were established more than 30 years ago and were never tied to inflation. In the early 1980s, $32,000 was a lot of income in retirement, so few were taxed. But, now that's hardly enough to live on. So, more recipients are subject to taxation. Very sneaky, congress!

When to Apply for Social Security

Okay, so Arnie and Lillian interviewed different advisors and asked each of them whether they should take Social Security now (now was a couple years ago, when they were 65 years old) or wait. Some advisors told them to take it now. Others said to wait. Here's the funny thing. None of these nimrods answered the question correctly since they had no contextual basis for making the statement. Not one of them knew anything about the couple or their resources. Therefore, the correct answer at the time would have been, "it depends." And, it does.

The decision of whether to begin receiving Social Security benefits at 62 or waiting until age 70 is entirely dependent upon other financial planning considerations, the most important of which are liquidity needs and taxes. For Arnie and Lillian, they had no liquidity constraints. Therefore, it made sense for them to postpone benefits. And, they were compensated for this. At age 70 they would receive 125% of what they would have gotten at full retirement age (66 years old). Putting off the benefit helped to keep their tax burden in check and the plan we developed for them included other techniques to further ensure that receiving the benefits didn't put them into an onerous tax position.

Now, with that said, for lots of people, taking Social Security at full retirement age (66 years old) instead of waiting until 70 makes sense. Sure, your benefit will be 24% greater if you wait the four years, but you will have missed out on four years of payments. If you don't need the money to live on and intend to invest your Social Security benefits, then bear in mind that the CAGR of that 25% over four years is 5.74%. That's a little more than half of what you could expect to earn if you took the benefit early and invested it in the S&P 500 over those same four years. But, unless your advisor has a handle on your entire financial picture, you could end up in a less advantageous place a few years down the road.

A Roth IRA Has the Exact Same Tax Benefits as a Regular IRA

Nope. Not right. Similar in one respect, but completely different in other ways. A Traditional IRA and a Roth IRA are similar in that they both allow the investments held in them to accumulate tax-free. That's it. That's all they have in common.

The first difference between the two is the tax treatment of the dollars you put into them. Both a Traditional IRA and a Roth IRA are funded with after-tax dollars (to begin with). After all, you write a check to get the money into either type of account.

The difference is that the money that goes into a Traditional IRA (for most people) is completely tax deductible. I say for most people because there are limitations on the deduction based on how much money you make. But, for most folks the contribution to a Traditional IRA is still completely tax deductible. This is not the case for a Roth IRA.

Contributions made to a Roth IRA are not deductible. There are also limitations on how much you can put into the account. And, again, those limitations are based on how much money you make.

The next difference between a Traditional IRA and a Roth IRA is that the money that comes out of the account (a distribution) is treated differently by the IRS. Distributions taken out of a Traditional IRA are taxable at your marginal rate. Distributions taken out of a Roth IRA are not taxed. And, this creates a nifty planning opportunity for many people.

IRS rules allow you to convert a Traditional IRA into a Roth IRA. Essentially, you pour the money out of the Traditional bucket into a Roth bucket. The distribution out of your Traditional IRA is taxed at your marginal rate the year you make the conversion. So, the planning opportunity comes when we know how your income will change over time.

A conversion can be made in a low-income year when the tax on the distribution won't throw you into a higher bracket. After that, the distributions out of the Roth IRA will not be taxed. The potential savings this planning technique provides come from the fact that in retirement you will forever avoid required minimum distributions, which would otherwise be taxable at your marginal rate. You pay the tax upfront, at conversion, enjoy years of tax-free compounding, and then get use of the money later in life with no future tax burden.

Required Minimum Distribution

Now, while we're on the subject of the RMD, let's explore another area where financial advisors disagree. Some say that the Required Minimum Distribution from your IRA can't be delayed. Others say that it can be. Technically, it can't be delayed. When you reach 70 ½ years of age the IRS requires you to start taking money out of your IRA. You can't defer the tax forever. Someone has to pay to keep the government running.

The year that you become 70 ½ is when you have to take that first taxable distribution. The reality is that you could take out as much as you like – and you'll pay taxes on whatever amount you withdraw. But, the IRS has a table that sets specific minimums that must come out beginning with that first distribution. The table is based on mortality rates, which are essentially the IRS's guess about how long people that age will keep living. The amount of your RMD is the result of applying the rates from the table to your IRA's value at the end of last year. That's pretty much it. It's cut and dry. This is the practical application of the old adage about death and taxes.

Under the right planning circumstances, however, it is possible to delay the RMD for up to 15 years. But, this is a technique that is really most appropriate for the septuagenarian who plans on working forever (well, at least until he or she is 85). The device that makes this happen is a Qualified Longevity Annuity Contract (QLAC).

In its simplest version (the more complicated applications aren't relevant to this book) a QLAC is essentially a deferred annuity purchased inside an IRA. There are limits imposed on how much of the IRA can be invested in one of these things as well as a bunch of rules and regulations governing their use. But, going into all that detail would just complicate this more, so I'll cut to the chase.

When a QLAC is used to defer the RMD, an investor must begin taking distributions absolutely no later than the very first day of the month following his or her 85th birthday – it's that specific! So, the planning for this has to be awfully precise. And, when these payments begin, they have to satisfy the RMD. The payments can't be less than the IRS table specifies. This presents another planning challenge. But, again, for guys like Mike Wallace and Morley Safer, who worked well into their 80s, the QLAC makes a lot of sense. They can also make sense in other circumstances.

For those with the resources, these annuities can be used to better match the timing of retirement income with liquidity needs. If liquidity doesn't become an issue until much later in life, then a QLAC might be a very appropriate vehicle to use to defer distributions until they're needed, while in the meantime the assets in the IRA grow tax-free.

The main risk of using a QLAC is that you die before your 85th birthday – and this happens to *lots* of Americans! If you do, then you've left a lot of money (RMDs that you didn't get to use) on the table. But, you'll be gone so does it matter?

The other risk is to your beneficiary. There's no "death benefit" from a QLAC. So, if you die before you reach 85, your heir gets just one of two things: either a lump sum equal to what you paid for the QLAC; or, the annuity payments you would have received from it. If you go after your 85th birthday, then the amount your beneficiary receives will be reduced by whatever annuity payments you got before you died.

The Required Minimum Distribution – Special Tax Considerations

When Arnie and Lillian were told that the RMD had no special tax considerations they weren't getting accurate information. The RMD can have either positive or negative effects depending upon whether or not the advisor plans properly.

One of the reasons that planning is so important is that investors who put off taking Social Security until age 70 also must begin taking RMDs at that time. The combination of the two can create an unexpected boost in taxable income and with it an increase in taxes. Without proper planning, that higher income can come with a commensurate bump up to the next tax bracket. This can be a shock. And, again, this is why planning is such a large part of our practice.

One planning opportunity using the RMD comes about because IRS rules say that you can use it to make charitable contributions. If you do this, then the distribution will not be taxable to you. What you give up is the tax deductibility of your charitable contribution. Hey, you can't have it both ways!

Using the RMD as a Qualified Charitable Distribution (QCD) lowers your income in the year you use it and can help you mitigate your tax burden. This is especially beneficial for taxpayers on the threshold of the next higher bracket. Planning strategies that use the RMD as a QCD can also help reduce the proportion of Social Security benefits that are subject to taxation, which I mentioned earlier, can be as high as 85%. Another benefit is that reducing taxable income also can eliminate the surcharge on Medicare premiums. One of the most important planning challenges related to the RMD is remembering to make it.

The planning work we did for Ned and Betsy Brainerd similarly helped them lower their tax bill.

The event that prompted the Brainerds to hire us was that their previous broker had failed to remind Ned that he had to take his RMD from his very substantial IRA. At the end of the year, the distribution wasn't taken. This was a really costly mistake! The penalty imposed for missing this one RMD was an additional 50% of Ned's required distribution. Ouch!

In general, there is no reprieve from this. But, we prepared an appeal on Ned's behalf and were able to work out a solution with the IRS that saved the Brainerds the penalty. It took a bit of work, and I can't say that the IRS would make such a concession in other circumstances, but I'm delighted that we could make this happen for them!

Sadly, I have seen other instances where someone has forgotten to make his or her RMD. It typically becomes an issue when a person moves an account from one firm to another and something falls through the cracks. The investor forgets, there is no notice from the custodian to take the distribution, and the RMD doesn't get taken that year. Because this can happen, we don't rely on custodians to provide our clients with notice.

Our firm takes a very proactive approach to making sure that snafus like this don't befall our clients. We're pretty hands-on. We remind them to take their RMDs, to file their returns or extensions on time, and to make their quarterly estimated tax payments, which can subject them to penalties if not filed in a timely fashion. Our goal is to make sure that we're not doing anything (or failing to do anything) that will put our clients in harm's way!

Now, let's look at what we did for Carol and Susan.

The couple's trading account generated a lot of short-term capital gains. In addition, the "safe" portion of their portfolio was invested in actively-managed mutual funds, which also spun off a lot of capital gains. And, then there was the fact that the stock-trading portion of their account generated a lot of commissions for the broker. What's more, the mutual funds cost them nearly 3% a year in fees and expenses. All of these were drains on their portfolio's net investment performance.

We have found that those advisors who encourage their clients to actively trade do so without regard for capital gains taxes. In the case of Carol and Susan, this was happening even though the broker was completely unaware of the couple's liquidity needs or other sources of income.

The solution for Carol and Susan was a relatively simple one. We prepared a plan that listed their specific consumption goals over the next five years and more loosely detailed their other many and various objectives at different stages of their lives after that. From there we prepared different schedules that laid out the funding requirements for those various goals. The different schedules detailed separate "what-if" scenarios.

The plan identified areas where some life insurance changes and estate plan updates made sense. It also identified how the couple could save money by making changes to their investment program. They stopped trading altogether and moved everything in the portfolio into a passive index-based growth and income strategy that more closely reflected their "goal funding" needs and risk tolerances. The result was that we helped them lower their tax bill and the cost of managing their investments.

The Bottom Line

Our perspective is that investors should not let the tail wag the dog. Proper planning can optimize one's tax situation over an extended period. And, there are robust tools and techniques that we use to do this.

We accept that taxes are never going to go away. The specific things on which the government levies them and the rates they charge will bounce around from one segment of our economy to another depending upon who wins elections between now and long after we're gone. In the meantime, our job is to understand the impact those changes will have on our clients and help them plan accordingly.

The fact of the matter is that all of our clients have to pay income taxes. There is no getting around this. So, that in and of itself is not a concern to us. Our concern is to make sure that we mitigate their effect on the bottom line for each client.

Sure, death and taxes are certain. But, as Will Rogers aptly said, *"The only difference between death and taxes is that death doesn't get worse every time Congress meets."*

CHAPTER 10

THE INN KEEPER & THE THIRD RAIL OF POLITICS

Quick! Before It's Too Late.

WE MET KATE Bradley at an educational seminar I was giving on Social Security. I have been teaching the subject for nearly a decade. She came up to me after the talk with a story about her former advisor, a stern curmudgeon who had spent a short time as an insurance salesman before becoming a broker. His name was Homer Bedloe. Kate went to Bedloe asking for help in deciding when to begin taking her Social Security benefits. He gladly supplied his suggestion. But, when Kate went to the local Social Security office with the same query, and to "fact check" his answer, she found out that the former insurance salesman's advice was completely wrong. When she confronted the perpetually grumpy Bedloe about it, his response was, "Yeah? Oh well."

Kate's a vivacious woman with the tiniest little voice. You'd swear that you were listening to Betty Rubble from the Flintstones when you hear her speak. She's a widower, and along with her three daughters, runs a small hotel, which is truly in the middle of nowhere. It rests in the shade of a railroad water stop roughly equidistant between two rural farming communities.

The question she posed to Bedloe was innocuous: "should I apply for Social Security benefits now or wait; and, if I wait, for how long?"

At 66 years old, Kate was at Full Retirement Age (FRA) according to the Social Security Administration's guidelines. So, she'd be entitled to unreduced retirement benefits. If she waited, her benefits would increase, but she certainly wasn't going to be penalized for taking them now. What she heard from Bedloe shocked her. After all, he was her financial advisor. He was a professional. He was (she thought) well-trained. He had to know the right answer.

"You better take Social Security now before it goes bankrupt," is what he said. And, he was absolutely serious!

Come on!

A potential bankruptcy of the Social Security system is not the *real problem* that investors face! The greater risk to individual investors isn't related to the balance of the Social Security trust fund or the cash flows into and out of it. It's not related to the mismatch between the number of baby boomers drawing from the fund and the smaller number of Gen-Xers and Millennials paying into it. It's not even related to Congress' continual pilfering from the trust fund.

The real problem that investors face regarding Social Security is that fewer than 30% of advisors have any knowledge of how it works. Most of them demonstrate a true lack of understanding of its intended purpose. They are not familiar with the function of its programs or any of their components. They don't know how it affects other sources of post-retirement income. They don't understand the impact of other sources of post-retirement income and they generally just don't want to be bothered! The reason for this last point is that it requires work to be able to understand Social Security and effectively incorporate it into a client's financial guidance. The problem most advisors have with that is that they can't earn a commission on it!

I'm not sure if Bedloe's dimwitted answer was just a snarky comment or if it was actually the broker's belief. Whichever it was, it clearly wasn't accurate – not by a long shot! I'll get to that later. For now, I want to address some of the other common delusions that people have about Social Security – many of which are perpetuated by a reckless media more bent on shocking its audience than informing it.

The Social Security Trust Fund Has Been Raided

This is the favorite rant of lunatics on both sides of the political aisle. The claim is that, in order to pay for some terrible partisan boondoggle, the President (whoever he is, from either party) has pilfered money from the Social Security trust fund. There are just two things wrong with this allegation.

The first is that the President doesn't have the ability to appropriate funds. Only the Congress does. Still, nearly every president since LBJ has been accused of stealing money from Social Security's surplus trust fund. Nixon is the one standout here. Go figure.

The second thing wrong with this assertion is that it doesn't add up. The math simply doesn't work! If nine of the last ten Presidents had taken money out of fund (to the degree that is alleged), then today there'd be no fund. But, making this distorted, spurious claim sells newspapers and keeps people glued to the Internet and their television screens.

The fact of the matter is that the balance of the trust reserve fund is merely an account on the books of the Department of Treasury. Revenues dedicated to the trust fund and benefit payments from it are merged with the Treasury's cash transactions for the rest of the government. The voices crying foul confuse cash flow management with misappropriation. They're not the same thing.

Social Security reserves are in effect "borrowed" for a time by the rest of the government and then repaid with interest when the trust fund needs them back. The net effect of this is exactly same as if Social Security's surplus was maintained separately from the rest of the government and invested in the open market. The trust fund doesn't gain or lose by the arrangement. It just makes managing cash flows easier.

Think of it this way. You may have separate bank accounts for your regular monthly living expenses, your "emergency fund", and your "vacation fund". The US government doesn't. If it did, the accounting would be a nightmare. So, there is no need to freak out. Nobody is stealing from Social Security.

Social Security Won't Exist for Young People

In a way, one could view this as being possible. But, its likelihood depends on a big "if". The continued existence of Social Security is completely dependent upon Congress. If they chose to scrap the program, then it wouldn't exist for future beneficiaries. Short of that, Social Security lives on. This is where the metaphor that Social Security is the third rail of politics speaks volumes.

Can you imagine any standing politician honestly arguing to eliminate Social Security? How successful do you think a legislator (let alone all 100 Senators and 435 Representatives) would be fighting to end the program? It would be the political equivalent to touching the middle rail of a subway track. And, just in case you don't live in a city that has a subway, the third rail is the one that carries the huge charge of electricity that powers the trains. Touch it and you're toast – quite literally!

So, with the exception of wishy-washy political rhetoric spewed at rallies to energize an entrenched base, there is not one honest voice in Washington (no pun intended) that would propose a bill to dismantle Social Security. It's just not going to happen. It would kill a politician's career just as surely as touching that third rail would.

If You Work While Taking Social Security – You Lose Your Benefits

First off, there is no such thing as "losing your Social Security benefits". There just isn't. You paid into the system now the system is there for you. And, no one can take Social Security away from you; period. But, scaremongers like to publish statements like this because it gets people's attention. So does yelling "fire" in a crowded theatre.

If you receive Social Security benefits while you're working and haven't yet reached Full Retirement Age (FRA), then you're going to receive a reduced amount. You're not going to lose your benefit. You're just not going to get 100% of it right then and there. How much of a reduction will be based on how old you are and how much you make. But, eventually, you'll get that all back.

As soon as you reach FRA, your benefits will be adjusted higher so that you get back what was previously withheld. For most folks, FRA means 66 or 67 years old. But, if you're already at Full Retirement Age, then you can work until the cows come home and it won't have any effect on your benefits. Just ask June Lockhart. She worked well into her 70s.

Social Security Is a Ponzi Scheme

Okay, first off, you have to be a very clever wordsmith to be able to weave a yarn that makes a reasonable case that the Social Security system is anything like a Ponzi scheme.

A Ponzi scheme is a criminal enterprise created to enrich a fraudster. The scam dupes investors by paying them off, not with the profits from a legitimate enterprise, but with the dollars coming in from new fraud victims. These schemes always collapse as later investors become scarce, leaving earlier ones holding the bag.

By contrast, Social Security is a social welfare program that ensures that working Americans don't end up destitute in retirement. It works because American people by-and-large are good caring individuals that don't want to see their fellow man suffer.

That may sound over-the-top, lofty, or even Pollyanna. But, the fact of the matter is that Social Security is a pact between generations that nearly all Americans – across party lines, age groups, race and ethnicity, and income levels – agree should be maintained. Most Americans understand that without Social Security, *they alone* would have to support their parents, grandparents, or other family members.

The prevaricators that want you to believe that Social Security is an evil government plot to "rob from Peter to pay Paul" say the same stupid thing about the credit multiplier effect (the ability for a bank to lend out to borrowers more money than it has on deposit from savers). They obviously don't have a clue about capitalism, free enterprise, or the American psyche.

Social Security is the most successful social welfare program ever devised by human beings because it has for generations kept vast numbers of Americans out of severe poverty. If you don't believe that creates a huge long-term benefit to society, then consider living in one of the hundreds of countries around the globe where such a safety net doesn't exist. Doesn't sound too appealing, does it? Social Security is one of the things that makes America great!

Suggesting that it is a Ponzi scheme because it is a pay-as-you-go system (where current contributors support the funding that pays out current recipients, who just happened to be previous contributors) is more than just an oversimplification. It's a dumb statement. What makes it even more inane is that it ignores the most basic aspect of the system.

The folks paying into the system do so by means of a tax. Some of them may grumble about the tax, but few disagree with its purpose. The important point here is that congress is not likely to repeal this tax! And, that gets me to what Homer Bedloe said to Kate Bradley.

Social Security Is Going Bankrupt

Social Security is not going bankrupt – no matter how strict a definition one uses for the term. Nobody currently receiving benefits is at risk of losing them and there is no risk in the short run that future retirees will be either. With that said, the Social Security Administration does admit that within the next 20 years, rising costs of the program will exceed the expected tax revenue that it brings in. That does not make the system insolvent!

Think about this in the context of your own household finances. If, in the course of preparing your regular budget you discovered that your expenses exceeded your income, what would you do? There really are only two courses of action. You can either rein in your spending or find additional sources of income.

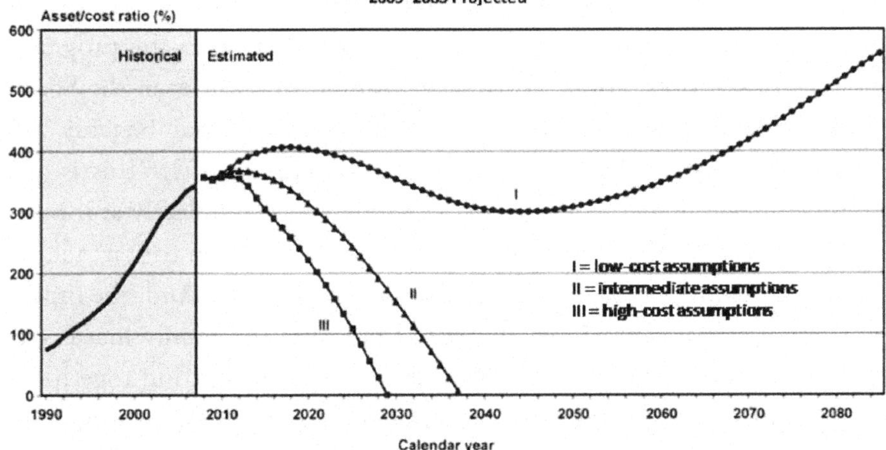

Source: 2009 Social Security Trustees Report, Figure II. D6 and Table IV. B3.

My sense is that lawmakers are not likely to suggest a reduction in benefits. That'd be like touching the third rail. They are much more likely to raise taxes to cover the shortfall. And, that's the point that the fear mongers seem to ignore. Social Security is funded by taxes.

Those taxes are paid by working people and their employers. In addition to that, some Social Security recipients themselves pay income tax on a portion of the benefits they receive. Congress has the power to manipulate all of these taxes. They could raise the rate paid by workers. They could raise the rate paid by employers. They could raise the income threshold for recipients, so that more of their benefits are taxed. That would make the pool of payers much bigger than it currently is. They could raise Full Retirement Age so that benefit payouts are delayed for future recipients. Or, they could do some combination of any or all of these.

In the final analysis, the fate of Social Security all boils down to this one important point. It relies on the full faith and credit of the United States. That's a creditor I'm comfortable with.

So What Should You Do?

Be careful. If you have questions about Social Security and are not sure that your current financial advisor is well versed in the program, then get a second opinion. And, bear in mind that not even the Social Security Administration can give you advice about your benefits (it's kind-of like asking the IRS a tax question…odd, isn't it?). This is one of those areas where the adage "trust but verify" is completely apropos.

There is a lot that goes into the decision about when to start taking benefits. Making the wrong choice can be a big mistake. And, the inputs are not just financial. There are a lot of personal and family matters to consider. Making the right decision is the result of putting together a number of seemingly unrelated yet interconnected pieces. Putting them together correctly will go a very long way to building a successful retirement plan. The Social Security component of this is confusing for many people – and for most of their financial advisors!

Part of the reason for this is that Social Security is different from what we have been taught about insurance. Traditional insurance protects us from the negative financial effect of an undesirable event: a flood; a fire; an accident; and, ultimately death. Oddly, Social Security provides financial protection of a different sort. It provides protection from the negative financial effect – not of dying too early – but of living too long. For many, this can be difficult to wrap their minds around.

That's why the extremely important decision about when to start taking benefits is so difficult to figure out. It is also why it should only be made in the context of a larger, holistic financial plan that takes into account the lifestyle you want to live, the cost to achieve that lifestyle over many years, and the sources of funds that will be required to finance it.

In every case, the key to using Social Security is to maximize your benefits. If you can do that, then you'll have more protection against running out of money later in life. Yet, sadly, most Americans don't. Fully 74% take their benefits early – before Full Retirement Age. Some do this out of necessity. But, others do it out of fear. And, that can lead to a bad decision.

That main thing you should do is have your financial advisor run a complete Social Security Analysis for you. If your advisor does not know how to prepare one, then you should consider switching advisors.

The Bottom Line

Put to rest the idea that Social Security is going to go bankrupt and focus on those things that you can control. Include a Social Security Analysis in your financial plan and tailor your investments around that to optimize each component vis-à-vis one another.

Ignore the banter about how bad off the Social Security system is and never forget the words of Franklin D. Roosevelt:

"...begin now to make provision for the future and that is why our Social Security program is an important part of the complete picture."

CHAPTER 11

POST-FEMINISM IN THE AGE OF RETIREMENT

The Frugal Breadwinner

MIRANDA HIXON IS a quiet, unassuming waif with mousy red hair and piercing green eyes. She's something of a cynic, but I guess many lawyers can be. She's retired now, but at one point in her career she was on track to become a partner at a high-profile New York City law firm.

Miranda was successful from the beginning of her career and was the first among her friends to buy her own home. Today, she and her husband Steve live in a modest townhouse in a trendy part of town. Miranda was the breadwinner when she and Steve were working and their not-inconsequential investment portfolio is the result of her earning power from years ago. But, the two have an almost austere lifestyle. They hardly spend any money at all. I'll get to the point of this later.

Don't Worry Be Happy

The reason I bring it up now is because it reminds me of something a stockbroker used to say to all of his clients back in the days when I was still very new in the business. He'd say, "Don't worry about having a shortfall when you retire. You will spend a lot less money after you stop working".

Really?

For many, this is a very accurate statement; but not for the reasons most advisors put forth. People spend less money in retirement because they have to; not because their expenses decrease. But, if your dream for retirement is to sit at home and watch television all day, then the old stockbroker's comment is true. You won't need much money to support that lifestyle. In reality, however, that isn't the type of retirement for which most people plan.

More likely, dreams of retirement include long trips to exotic locations, short trips to familiar spots to visit with family and friends, long leisurely weekends bothering your children and spoiling their kids, working in the garage building useless things out of wood or quilting and knitting articles that people you care about dread getting for Christmas. Maybe retirement means a boat and a house on the lake. Maybe it's that old car you lusted after as a kid but couldn't afford until now. Maybe it's nothing material.

Perhaps retirement means near-full time work without pay, like volunteering at the hospital or an animal shelter. Perhaps retirement is the time that you actually get to sit down and write that novel you've always had secretly tucked away in your head. Or, it could simply be staying up until midnight with the one you love watching movies and reruns of old television shows; and then, staying in bed the next morning in a room that doesn't have an alarm clock in it. Maybe it's a combination of some or all of this kind of stuff.

Whatever one's dream of retirement is, the common thread that weaves through the lives of nearly all retirees is that all of a sudden, the clock and the calendar are no longer in control of their lives. Retirement is the time when time doesn't matter. You can use it as productively or waste it as frivolously as you want. Not since you were in elementary school have ever been able to do all the things you want to do – all the things that you never seemed to have enough time to do before. And, now, the only limiting factor is money.

Even if none of the things I listed above appeal to you, the fact of the matter is that any difference between your pre-retirement and post-retirement living expenses is not likely to be big. In fact, most retirees see a decrease of no more than 20%. In other words, if your annual living expenses are $45,000 while you're working, then you can reasonably expect that they will be right around $36,000 in retirement. And, this doesn't include any of the stuff I described above. Those would be extras (look, cable TV isn't free)!

I'm going to stray here for a moment and recount a conversion I recently had with a neighbor of mine. She's older than I am. Her kids have long since left the house and have children of their own. Her daughter, who was a stay-at-home mom, is going through a pretty nasty divorce right now. According to my neighbor, the soon-to-be "X", who is a pretty successful businessman and who controlled the purse strings, has essentially cut her off financially. What a jerk! My neighbor has had to step in and for the time being help support her daughter and grandchildren.

Now, I want to get back to the discussion of your living expenses in retirement. Your new baseline "monthly nut" is going to be about 80% of what it was while you were working. This means that if you plan to have any fun (like travel), then you're going to have to replace that lost income.

Oh, another thing to consider as you get older – and the odds are good that you'll live another 20 to 30 years in retirement – is that your healthcare costs are going to rise at about twice the rate of inflation. So, you're going to want to make sure that you have enough tucked away to be able to keep up with the rising cost of medical care and prescription drugs. The reason for this is that as we get older, we need more stuff like that! And, don't forget that since you won't be working, your employer won't be paying for your insurance. So, add that to the budget. And, remember, Medicare is not free!

Now, don't forget the story about my neighbor, her daughter, and that jerk that left her. If you have kids, then you need to be prepared for the possibility that they (or their children) may need some financial support at some point in time. So, the notion that you shouldn't worry and be happy because you'll spend less money in retirement than you did while you were working is nonsense.

The Spendthrift's Closet

Miranda has a friend named Carrie Bushnell, who is also a client of ours. Carrie is a glamorous woman with a long narrow face and long narrow arms attached to a long narrow torso. She is gazelle-like in her movement and her flowing gingery blonde mane whips from side to side across the small of her back as she strides gracefully down the street. Carrie's poise is remarkable. It's as if invisible strings attached to the bottom of her spine and the top of her head keep her perpetually perpendicular to the ground. Her gait is confident. Her typically brand-new Manolo Blahniks strike the pavement with the precision of a tightrope walker, one precisely in front of the other, with each step. Carrie and Miranda are about the same age but Carrie is still working. She has to be.

Carrie's life is now, and always has been, a little bit more about form than substance. Don't get me wrong, she is a terrific woman and fun to be around. She's just a bit cavalier. When she was young and working at her first job she would buy Vogue magazine instead of dinner. Even years later, after some success had come her way, she once spent so much money on shoes that she didn't have enough for a deposit on a new apartment.

Carrie has a unique style sense and her closet is festooned with pieces by Armani, Versace, Valentino, Schiaparelli, Chanel, and Dior. And, that's why she's still working and likely will be well into her early 70s. She's not at risk of living out of a shopping cart and eating cat food. Carrie does make a lot of money. Unfortunately, she is paying a price now for not saving earlier. That price is a late retirement.

The Fast and the Frivolous

I bring this up because it reminds me of another dopey thing I hear other financial advisors say to clients. "Spend more in early retirement to have fun!"

This ill-conceived baloney is horrible advice! It would be disastrous for someone in Carrie's situation to follow this kind of reckless recommendation. And, it would be nearly as calamitous for the average retiree. This is the kind of cockamamie counsel that uninformed financial advisors offer to people when they don't have a clue about the client's broader financial picture. What makes these types of blanket statements so irresponsible is that the life expectancy of most retirees increases with every passing year! Frivolous spending in the early years of retirement would jeopardize one's safety net. And, any remaining funds would be consumed by inflation faster than Ms. Pac-Man can eat a maze full of pellets. What's worse, depleting retirement assets early would leave no wiggle room for unexpected contingencies. You can only spend a dollar once. When you do, it's gone. And, it's gone forever! Once retirement funds are exhausted, the only solution is to go back to work.

So What Should You Do?

I am going to explain one of our key planning philosophies in the context of how it specifically applies to Miranda and Carrie and in so doing will make the broader point about the economic concept of utility.

One sees a bittersweet irony when Miranda and Carrie's situations are viewed next to one another. Miranda was a saver from long ago; Carrie, not so much. Miranda's behavior set her up so that now, in retirement, she and her husband have the wherewithal to accomplish any financial goal they desire. Carrie has to keep working, and will have to restrain her spending after retirement. Miranda is in a position where she can almost spend freely without blowing the budget, whereas Carrie has to monitor her monthly nut very closely. Here's the irony.

Miranda and Steve are perfectly content staying in the neighborhood and spending small amounts of money on their regular coffee dates, lunches, and dinners. They are happy patronizing the local shops to buy knick-knacks and doodads with which they spoil their son Brady's children. Vacations are spent with family, which is their greatest indulgence. They lavish them with gifts and treat them to wonderful dinners and shared evenings out. While Miranda and Steve are likely to live for decades to come, they will still end up leaving a generous estate to Brady and his family.

Carrie's situation is a little different. She is going to consume the majority of her estate all by herself...which is okay since she is divorced and has no children. Carrie is a world traveler and has been everywhere; Paris, Abu Dhabi, you name it. And, she enjoyed those trips without regard to their cost. She didn't care about their expense at the time because she could afford it on her salary. But, she also didn't consider their future cost in terms of the number years of retirement she could have enjoyed if she had only forgone a few of those trips.

The same can be said of her closet full of designer everything. Each dress she owns represents a lost opportunity to compound her money. Every pair of Walter Steiger or Christian Louboutin shoes could easily have funded an annual IRA contribution, which today could have provided her tens-of-thousands of dollars in additional savings. Instead she has a closet worthy of spread on the pages of Elle magazine. The moral of those stories is this.

Money truly has no value unless it is used. What one uses it for is where all the value lies. The price tag for the things that matter to Miranda and Steve are not very big at all. But, to them the value of those simple things is enormous. For Carrie, a closet full of the latest designer fashions is the highest and best use of her money. Not much else (except maybe wearing those outfits as she saunters along the Champs-Élysées) would have any use for her.

The link between the two is that the price tag doesn't matter for either Miranda or Carrie. What does matter is the joy the respective thing brings to the respective purchaser. This is what is meant by the term "utility" as it is used by economists. What is important to one person may not be to another. And, that "importance" all boils down to how useful the thing is to that specific consumer. That usefulness may be how much someone enjoys a thing. It may also be a how a thing makes someone feel. The value of a dollar isn't that it is a dollar. A dollar's value comes from what you can do with it.

For example, Miranda and Steve wouldn't have any interest in a Gucci handbag. And, that would be the case even if they could buy one at Target for twenty bucks. A trip to Paris would only be pleasant for them if they could haul the entire family along with them. Conversely, Carrie's stroll along the Champs-Élysées wouldn't be at all pleasurable to her if she was weighed down by a throng of relatives. And, that would be the case even if she could fly the whole brood there on a private jet and put them all up in the penthouse suite of the Hôtel Fouquet's Barrière for those same twenty bucks.

The utility value of a dollar plays a key role in the planning advice we offer to clients. We ask each of them to take an honest look at the life they want to live. We get them to focus – not so much on the dollars and cents – but on their hopes, goals, wants, and dreams. We ask them to be reflective and to think about what's *REALLY* most important to them. For some, their greatest desire is to spoil their grandchildren. For others, it is traveling around the world. Others feel that covering the cost of health care, including long-term and catastrophic care, is of paramount importance. But, whatever the specific goals are, in the final analysis we always relate them back to money and its utility.

Our goal is to help our clients determine what the cost of their hopes, goals, wants, and dreams will be in retirement. The reason for this is that most people have to make trade-offs. So, prioritizing goals is important. That's why we ask every client what they *REALLY* want to spend their money on. A dollar can only go so far and our goal is to help our clients manage their financial affairs in a way that offers them the highest probability of attaining their most important goals.

The Bottom Line

Retirement presents a number of unique challenges. People's retirement incomes are typically lower than the wages they earn while working.

There aren't any "raises" in retirement (hence the catchy phrase, living on a fixed income). However, living expenses don't decease a whole lot. And, all retirees enter this stage of their lives with finite resources.

What makes all of this challenging is that it requires that people be conscientious savers during their working years. It also necessitates rigorous financial planning to make sure that one's savings are sufficient to ultimately finance his or her retirement goals. And, then after all is said and done, retirees have to pick carefully among the things they want to achieve in order to increase the likelihood that their highest priority goals don't get sacrificed to some unexpected expense.

A good way to keep all of this in perspective is to heed the advice offered by William Faulkner when he said, *"I say money has no value; it's just the way you spend it."*

CHAPTER 12

FATHER'S BROKER KNOWS BEST

YOU HAVE PROBABLY guessed it by now. Most of our firm's clients are women. That was our vision at the outset. But, it is also the result of a little serendipity. We have a strong bond with our clients and we just seem to click with them. Serving other women suits us and we feel that we have a unique perspective into what makes them tick. We believe we do a pretty good for our clients and thankfully that's the feedback we get from them.

So far in this book I have described a number of client situations and explained how we helped each person deal with them. Most of the vignettes I presented were about women. But, the types of solutions we provided to those clients aren't gender specific. The principals and the methods discussed so far work just as well for men as they do for women. This chapter is just slightly different.

These last two stories are about something that really boils my blood. These two stories recount something we have heard over and over again. What kills me is that it's still happening, now, in the 21st century!

Really?

Keep It in the Family

Kathy Anderson didn't change her last name when she married Dr. Jason Harper. I mention this only because Jason's stockbroker, Ed Davis, was the same advisor that Kathy's father, Jim, had been using for years. I think Jim may actually have introduced the two men. The reason this is important to the story is that even though Ed had met Kathy a zillion times (the Davis family lived down the street from the Andersons), he never made the connection that she was married to Dr. Harper.

When Kathy's father passed away a number of years ago, he left her with a small inheritance. Jim's total estate was evenly divided between Kathy and her older siblings, Betty and James, Jr. Father, as the kids called Jim when they were growing up, had been in the insurance business. So, he had a pretty good understanding of estate planning. The assets that each of the kids inherited was held in separate irrevocable trusts.

Because an irrevocable trust isn't a marital asset (even in a community property state) Kathy and Jason agreed that she should meet with Ed Davis on her own to decide what to do with the stocks in the account. That meeting didn't go so well.

"I went into that meeting with an open mind," Kathy told me, as she began to recount the story.

She said that Ed told her he was happy she had decided to keep the money with him and that it was, "certainly the right thing to do".

"I was your dad's advisor so I should be yours too. You loved your dad, right? Well, this was his legacy to you. There's a little bit of your dad's soul in this portfolio and that's why I don't want you to do anything with these stocks. That would be like getting rid of your dad's dog. It'd just be wrong."

"But, some of these stocks have been in the portfolio for thirty years. I've researched them. Most of them are not the same companies they were when Father bought them. The research I've seen suggests that they won't be the same companies twenty years from now, when I'll need the money," was Kathy's response. Kathy was savvy about money. She had been since she was a little kid.

"Listen Kitten," Ed barked back. "Don't confuse the roles here. My job is to do the research, pick the stocks, and help you out by telling you when to buy or sell them. Your job is to sit back and enjoy the dividend income I'm generating for you."

Kathy and Jason came into our office the very next day. A week later, after all of the accounts transferred over to our custodian, Ed called Jason and asked what prompted him to move his account to another advisor. "'Kitten' thought it was a good idea," was his reply.

Don't Worry Princess

Betty Donohue had been married to Jerry twelve years before he passed away. He left her with two young daughters, a life insurance policy, a comfortable 401 (k) that had to be rolled over into an IRA, and an investment portfolio of stocks, bonds, and mutual funds. While there would be enough resources for Betty to raise the girls, Jenny and Ellen, and send them to college, the one-time housewife would now have to go back to work.

But, before that, there was the meeting with the broker. And, this one didn't go so well either. Here's what Betty told me happened when she went into the broker's office.

"His demeanor was more somber than the guy at the mortuary that arranged Jerry's funeral. It was almost theatrical. 'Your husband was a Prince. Everybody loved him.' was what he told me. I'm sure they hardly knew each other. Then, he actually leaned forward and grasping his hands condescendingly said that he understood that I 'didn't understand much about investments' and that he 'would take good care of' me. I was never so insulted".

Wow! I can almost hear what that broker must have been thinking: *Don't worry your pretty little head about finance and numbers!*

Seriously? Are we living in a Gone with the Wind movie?

Look, I worked at a "Wall Street" firm in the 1980s and I know what the culture was back then. It was part frat-house, part high school boys' locker room. The women that worked in support roles were objectified and the women who worked as brokers or traders we despised and disrespected. Even the women who were clients didn't get a break. They were treated kindly, but mostly as empty-headed children who had to be instructed about their finances. But, the boys really knew how to lay it on thick when they could smell opportunity. And opportunity meant commissions!

Tugging on a woman's heartstrings while she was grieving never failed the boys in the bullpen. They could get a mourning widow to turn over an entire portfolio in a moment of weakness. I've heard the story a thousand times. The amazing thing to me is that today this is still ubiquitous in the financial services industry!

And, the pitch is pretty much the same as what both Kathy and Betty heard: *You are in good hands; I'll take care of you; you grieve, I'll take care of your money; trust me, I'm a professional.*

Yeah. They'll take care of you alright. Don't be fooled.

What you get with your dad's broker is your dad's old-fashioned, high-priced portfolio. We see this frequently. A client inherits money from a relative and the makeup of that inheritance is some combination of stocks, bonds, mutual funds, and money market holdings. The mix is never the same. That mix, whatever it is, may have been appropriate for the person from whom it was inherited, but it may not be suitable for the beneficiary. If a broker is responsible for that portfolio's construction, then he or she may be reluctant to dismantle their creation just because your investment objectives are different from your benefactor's.

Much has changed over the last 50 years in the way investment professionals view portfolio theory and investment strategy. Ideas that were considered radical in the 1970s are mainstream thought today. When the notion of a passive (unmanaged) mutual fund pegged to track the performance of the S&P 500 index was introduced, it was regarded as folly. Today, there are about $3 trillion dollars in such funds.

The services provided by a broker have also changed. Prior to 1975, brokerage firms provided just one service; help buying or selling shares of stock or individual bonds. Today, an individual investor can expect so much more from a broker that the line between securities salesman and financial advisor has blurred to the point of invisibility.

These factors are a huge part of how the cost of financial advice has also changed over that same period of time.

So What Should You Do?

Individual investors that enjoy the benefit of a sudden windfall need to be careful. This is especially the case if that instant payday is the result of an inheritance. Inherited money held at a brokerage firm may come along with an incumbent broker as part of the package. And, that broker may have an attachment to your newfound wealth. He or she may feel entitled to it remaining at his or her firm, under his or her control. But, remember, whether or not it does, is entirely up to you!

I'm not suggesting that all incumbent financial advisors be summarily fired. I am merely suggesting that you perform some meaningful due-diligence before you make a commitment. As every smart woman knows, it pays to shop around.

As you go shopping, look at the former advisor anew; treat the old incumbent like everyone else you interview. Don't give him or her any special consideration. While the ultimate goal is to find someone who fits with your personality, it should only be the deciding factor if everything else is equal. More importantly, you're shopping for a fiduciary who will act in your best interest. As you interview potential advisors you are going to have to ask some tough questions. Remember, this is a business decision, not a personal one. Here are some of the questions we expect potential clients to ask us…and what we make sure to tell them if they don't:

- *How long have you been in this business?*
- *Tell me about your previous employers and experience.*
- *What licenses do you hold?*
- *What certifications have you attained?*
- *What credentials have you earned?*
- *What professional associations are you a member of?*

- *What entities regulate your business?*
- *Have you ever been the subject of a customer complaint?*
- *Have you ever been the subject of a regulator's inquiry?*
- *How many clients do you have?*
- *How many assets do you oversee?*
- *What is your average account size?*
- *What is your account minimum?*
- *Who is your typical client?*
- *What is your specialty?*
- *What is your primary service offering?*
- *What ancillary service do you provide?*
- *Will you be my sole advisor or will I work with a team?*
- *If I will work with a team, what roles will each member play?*
- *How are you compensated?*
- *Who will manage my money?*
- *How will my money be managed?*
- *What is your investment philosophy?*
- *What is your investment methodology?*
- *What discretion will you have over my account?*
- *Where will my money be held – who is the custodian?*
- *How will you communicate with me?*
- *How often will you communicate with me?*
- *What forms of communication can I expect to get from you?*

You'll likely have more than one meeting with each of the advisors you interview. But, as you winnow the pack down to just a few finalists, it'll be time to ask one of the most important questions. This should be one of the last things to ask and should be asked only of those advisors you are convinced are the final two or three candidates. At the end of your vetting process, ask each advisor for the names and contact information of three current clients that you can talk with. Don't hire anyone without talking with at least three references.

The last thing to do before you sign the transfer documents is to go online and look up the advisor on www.brokercheck.com. If you have asked all of the questions above and received (honest) answers that meet your satisfaction, then the results of the background check will confirm that.

This is a big decision, so you have to get it right the first time. If you do, then you will be engaged in a long-term business relationship with this advisor. Getting this decision right can reap many financial benefits for years to come. Just remember that you want to make sure that the person you hire is going to provide you with the services that are important to you.

The Bottom Line

Inherited money is nice; an inherited broker, not so much. That's why it pays to shop around. Inheriting money is only one reason why you might go looking for a new financial advisor. But, whatever the reason for the search, the process should be the same. Looking for a financial advisor is not easy. How you go about finding the right fit for you is important. If you click with your advisor, that's great! Just make sure that you're clicking with a qualified fiduciary.

And, when you do go looking, we'd suggest that you follow the advice of Vivian Wood, the villain portrayed by Kelly Lynch in the movie remake of the old television show Charlie's Angels. In one of the movie's opening scenes she says to her partner in crime, *"Never send a man to do a woman's job"*.

We couldn't agree more!

ADDENDUM

FINANCIAL WELLNESS FOR LIFE

OKAY, I HAVE pointed out throughout this book that the investment planning and management work we do for clients does not occur in a vacuum. Every financial decision we help clients work through is considered in the context of a holistic financial and life plan that is unique for each individual client. Our main role as advisors is to make sure that assets are allocated and the right decisions are made so that they have the freedom to live the life they want to live.

Every choice clients make when they spend money will have an impact on their long-term finances. At this point, I want to mention that this first phase of the planning process doesn't have anything to do with money. It's all about getting to know clients as people. We want them to be introspective about what is important to them. We want to understand what makes them tick. Before we give counsel, we talk with them about their hopes, goals, wants, and dreams. We ask clients to tell us about the things that they'd like to do before retirement and the things they'd like to do after retirement. We talk with them about what they'd like to achieve on a personal level. We talk about family, community, and charity. We get our clients to consider their place on Earth and explain what they want to accomplish while they're here.

There are a couple reasons for this. The first is that this exercise helps clients visualize their goals in a way that they may never have previously, so they see them in a whole new light. The second reason is that this helps to prioritize the action that needs to be taken to create the life they want to live.

Our planning methodology is all about guiding our clients to articulate what's important to them so that we can begin to build the foundation for making the right decisions to reach as many of their high-priority goals as possible. Understanding what is important helps us (essentially) price their goals. By putting a price tag on our clients' many and various objectives we help them see what is possible to achieve using only the assets they currently have available. It also allows us to show them what might be possible over time as the value of their assets grows. This exercise helps our clients' transition from thinking about their goals subjectively to viewing them in the context of how much money it will take to actually see them come to fruition. This becomes the foundation of the plan.

After that, the conversation becomes money-centric as we begin to collect data on issues ranging from whether the client has a proper amount saved in an emergency fund to whether or not they are borrowing money efficiently. Our questions in this phase of the planning process focus on things like funding their tax deferred retirement plan, optimizing income taxes, and evaluating insurance coverage.

From here we fold longer-term financial considerations into the conversation. What are the client's estate planning objectives? Is a durable power of attorney in place? Has the couple spelled out health care directives? Is there a will or a trust? Have the proper beneficiaries of insurance and retirement accounts been named? After this, the initial framework of the client's financial plan begins to take shape.

We counsel our clients to think of their spending decisions in the context of their current net worth as if it were a closed economy. We ask them to think about every spending decision as if it were a "guns or butter" trade-off. You can spend a dollar only once. And, after it is spent, it's gone. So, as part of the planning process we ask each client if they really know how much money they actually have, how much they save, and how much they spend every year. After which we help them get their arms around the mathematics of their current financial situation.

Holistic financial planning is an iterative process. It reveals its optimal structure after many conversations. As this takes place with each client, we develop a series of "what-if" scenarios taking each of their highest-priority goals into consideration so that they can evaluate various alternative courses of action and funding plans. As the years progress, this plan will change because life happens and change is inevitable.

As I mentioned in Chapter One, the plan is the result of yet another fact-finding conversation, much of it focused on risk tolerance. In this phase of the planning process we also discuss the necessity of matching the time horizon of various investments with specific goals. It is appropriate to finance long-term goals with long-term financial assets.

For example, if sending your three kids to college in 14, 16, and 18 years is one of your goals, then using assets that are likely to achieve their highest return potential over 14 to 18 years are the most appropriate to use for funding. The planning work we do takes this notion a step further. If a lump sum is not available today to plunk down and set aside for up to eighteen years, then our planning approach will include information about how a gradual accumulation over time can help meet those future funding requirements by using a dollar-cost-averaging approach over a long period of time. And, in general, this regular funding routine will be invested in a diversified portfolio of assets that meet the appropriate level of risk. We follow this same approach as we address every one of the client's life goals. This is, in essence, informed cash flow management and it happens throughout life.

The plans we develop for clients are not huge, leather-bound tomes. They are precise, concise guides that contain the client's specific life objectives juxtaposed against a macro overview of the financial strategies – including assets and liabilities – that will be deployed over time in the pursuit of achieving those goals. The plans make specific recommendations but, they are not cast in stone. By design, the plans we create for clients are intended to be flexible to adapt to changes in the client's personal life. For this reason, we regularly meet with each client to review and reevaluate his or her plan to make sure that the roadmap retains its value taking into consideration the twists and turns that alter circumstances.

Our perspective is that investors should not make any important financial decision in the absence of a holistic plan. This includes, but is not limited to, whether to buy or sell a long-term asset or whether or not to borrow money to make a purchase or to make an investment. It also includes the decision of whether or not to make a particular investment that might offer some specific special attribute, from a high yield or a tax advantage (remember, if something sounds too good to be true, it usually is).

Our role is to help clients see what is most appropriate in the context of their unique individual situation. We strive to coach our clients in a way that allows them to think about their resources in the context of their many and varied lives; including financial, personal, and philanthropic. Then, we implement these plans within a structure that mitigates fees over the long-term and positions investments to maximize their effectiveness.

Over the long term, we continue to advise adjustments to clients as their unique personal circumstances change over time. As our clients' lives unfold, we work with them to ensure that the plan in place does not become stagnant. What is appropriate today for a couple in their twenties with no children will be dramatically different as they have kids, raise them, send them off to college, marry them off, and then downsize and retire. Our job is to make sure that each transition in those lives is financed efficiently and optimally.

The single most important piece of advice we offer our clients was best summed up by Benjamin Franklin when he said, *"If you fail to plan, you are planning to fail"*!

AUTHOR BIO

Lorraine Ell
CEO and Senior Financial Advisor
Better Money Decisions, a Registered Investment Advisory firm

LORRAINE ELL is the CEO of Better Money Decisions (B$D) and Better Insurance Decisions. As co-owner of B$D, she is excited to continue her long career as an investment professional which started when she worked in the 1980s as an advisor with Drexel, Burnham and Lambert and J.W. Charles and as Co-owner of a Registered Investment Advisory (RIA) firm.

Lorraine is the only advisor in New Mexico who holds the Chartered Federal Employee Benefits Consultant designation (ChFEBCsm). She provides comprehensive financial and retirement management to federal employees. "Being able to maximize the complex and confusing maze of federal benefits will lead to a successful retirement. Those who think they can do it themselves often lack the holistic, long-term view that we provide. One mistake in early retirement can have a butterfly effect that lasts a lifetime."

Solving challenging financial problems for clients is Lorraine's most important role. "Wealth management oversight requires vast knowledge and expertise since every aspect of a person's life has a financial component. Clients come to me with questions such as how to handle restricted stock, what to do about an annuity they were sold and don't want, or which way to finance or pay for a new house, car or education. The answers are unique for everyone."

Her international experiences, from teaching in Saudi Arabia to co-founding a marketing company in Budapest, Hungary, gives her a unique perspective in creating a better financial services firm guiding clients from multiple cultures to financial wellness for life. "I want B$D to be responsive to what clients really need and that differs from person to person. Tired clichés and pat answers do not help most people make better decisions."

Lorraine also lived in Tehran before and during the 1978 and 1979 revolution. "What I learned from that experience is that risk can change at any time. One moment the city streets are bustling with people living their daily lives and then, in a flash, there is chaos." Managing risk is a hallmark of the advice the firm provides.

As a lifelong entrepreneur, Lorraine has worked in a variety of industries including financial services, education and health & beauty. "I have had a life full of exciting adventures and I now want to help others manage their assets so they are able to live their dreams." Her vast entrepreneurial experience enables her to help small business owners successfully retire.

You will find her cooking for friends and family on the weekends, especially Italian food and it should come as no surprise that she is a Past Chair of the Albuquerque Committee on Foreign Relations and is a member of a policy group called Wednesday's Women. She visits her sons and grandchildren at every opportunity.

LORRAINE'S BETTER MONEY DECISION: Taking a trip around the world after working in Saudi Arabia despite the cost and time. An unforgettable experience!

LORRAINE'S MONEY MISTAKE: Splitting the rent on an office space with another business owner. Guess who ended up paying for it all!

GET YOUR FREE BONUS

FIND OUT IF it's time for you to switch to a fee-only fiduciary.

DOWNLOAD THE BONUS report:
"SEVEN WARNING SIGNS you are working
with the wrong advisor!"

VISIT WWW.BOZOSMONSTERSWHIZBANGS.COM

Made in the USA
Columbia, SC
02 March 2018